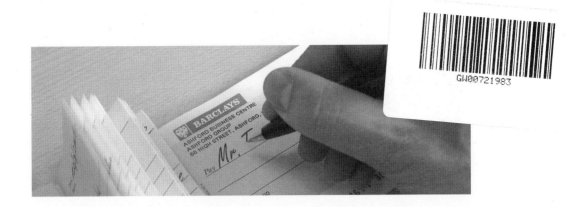

Getting the company to pay

indicator

ISBN 0-9552070-2-9

ISBN 978-0-9552070-2-0

First Edition - Third print - E1P3

Table of contents

5. Use of home by a company

6. Garden maintenance

7. Gifts

8. Language lessons

9. Magazine subscriptions

10. Paying for a holiday

11. Private tutors

12. School fees

13. Personal trainer

14. Cars for the family

15. Wine

16. Company plane (or yacht)

17. Gym membership

18. Garage storage

19. Nannies

20. Petty cash differences

21. The weekend away

22. Domestic help

23. Taxi fares

24. Overnight allowance

25. Use of the company villa

26. Advisors' fees

27. Parking near work

28. Entertaining

29. Computer equipment

30. Technical notes

1. Introduction

1.1. HOW TO USE THIS BOOK

This book sets out, clearly and in one place, the ground rules for legitimately putting expenses through your business. Remember, the Taxman only ever gives you his biased interpretation. You'll be able to clearly see how much you could save by putting an expense through your company rather than paying for it yourself. All the taxes are brought into the equation, it's the full story, with no "too good to be true" nasty surprises later.

Why would you want to put expenses through your business anyway? You'll find the answers to this in Chapter 1 which also lays down the basis on which any expense can be legitimately claimed.

How to interpret these rules to your legitimate advantage in a company situation comes next in Chapter 2, together with some very practical dos and don'ts.

If you're self-employed or have additional freelance income, the ground rules are a little different, requiring a different approach if you're to get the best out of them. So for completeness we've covered this in Chapter 3.

You can keep the Taxman in check in Chapter 4. This ranges from answering questions such as "How will the Taxman know?" to getting your paperwork and figures spot on and providing you with responses to an enquiry.

In Chapters 5 to 29 you'll be able to pick up on new angles, with ideas you may not otherwise have thought of plus advice on how to implement them.

Backing you up is Chapter 30. This is your own expenses databank with technical sources for the advice in the book and suggestions as to where you might want to go next for help with any documentation.

1.2. WHY PUT EXPENSES THROUGH MY BUSINESS?

Ask any entrepreneur and they'll tell you that their primary motivation for setting up in business is to make a profit. In fact, the profit motive is one of the tests used by the Taxman to determine whether an activity can be genuinely classed as a "trade" as opposed to an "investment" activity.

Profit is generated by the maximisation of sales revenues and the minimisation of costs. Unfortunately, for almost every pound earned in profit there will be taxes to pay in one form or another, and whilst the majority of us accept that taxation is inevitable we also want to keep our liabilities to a minimum.

One way to do this is to simply earn less profit in the first place, but this defeats the object of going in to business; nobody sets out to be unsuccessful. But it is possible to reduce taxable profits by increasing your tax deductible expenses. You could achieve this by finding new ways to spend your money; maybe renting flash offices or holding lavish parties for your customers. Maybe you could charter a yacht for your next business meeting?

We can all think of ways to spend money. An office suite with an upmarket address makes good business sense if it will attract more and better business. However, if you can take some of your day-to-day "personal expenditure" and convert it into "business expenditure" that can be charged against tax, you can achieve your goal of reducing your taxes and keeping more of the profit for yourself.

1.2.1. How will I be better off?

Let's take this simple scenario as an example:

Example

Robert's business makes £50,000 profit each year. The Taxman's slice is £20,000, which leaves £30,000 for Robert, all of which he spends. His computation looks like this:

	£
Profit	50,000
Tax charge @ 40%	(20,000)
Retained profit available	**30,000**

If Robert could charge a proportion of the £30,000 he spends to the business, then his tax bill would go down. Let's say £5,000 can be charged against his profits in this way. His new computation looks like this:

	£
Original profit	50,000
Less: additional expenses	(5,000)
Revised profit	45,000
Revised tax charge @ 40%	(18,000)
Retained profit available	27,000
Add: additional expenses	5,000
Total available	**32,000**

Now Robert has an extra £2,000 available to him, which is basically the reduction in his tax bill from £20,000 to £18,000. Although his accounting profit has gone down, his spending power has gone up.

1.2.2. Can I charge everything to my company/business?

In an ideal scenario we would charge every penny we spend against the business and pay no taxes at all, but this is obviously unrealistic. The Taxman may be a lot of things, but he isn't a fool. After all, if you were to consistently show losses on your tax returns but lived a privileged lifestyle, then before you could say "Lester Piggott" he'd start making a few enquiries!

The reality is that for most owner-managers the line between their private and business lives is so blurred that you can't always tell where one ends and the other begins. With some things it's more obvious than others, like the company car for example, which clearly has both business and personal uses. Others are not so straightforward. For example, how many people take work home with them? If the accounts are done on the kitchen table, is the cost of heating and lighting that room attributable to business or private use? What about telephone calls, or using the Internet for research? How many people pick up bits and pieces for the office along with the groceries? Does that make it a business trip? And that newspaper you read every morning with the business section...?

The list could go on, but the point is clear: there are times when what we naturally think of as household expenses also have a work-related element to them. These can, in part or in whole, be quite legitimately charged against profit.

But don't be fooled into thinking you can take liberties with the tax rules. There are clear principles that have to be followed for the expense claim to be considered legitimate by the Taxman. A quick review of the rules will demonstrate why.

1.2.3. How much can I save?

<u>Incorporated</u>

The question many people will be asking at this stage is whether the amount saved in tax will be worth the extra hassle of making the claim, particularly for those of us who aren't over keen on paperwork.

> *<u>Example</u>*
>
> *Imagine you can turn £50 per month into business expenses. That's £600 per year, and at a tax rate of 19%, this will save your company £114*

in Corporation Tax. And that's not all, because you have just saved the company the equivalent in salary costs for you of £600 net of tax. The tax and NI bill on the gross equivalent is £417 for you and another £130 for the company, making £661 saved all together. Now it starts to look like a good proposition!

Unincorporated

For an unincorporated business it's much simpler to work out the savings. If you're paying tax at 40%, then with the Class 4 NI supplement of 1% to consider the overall saving is £246. This may not look particularly attractive when compared with the limited company savings, but as we touched on earlier it's far easier to charge expenses against profit as a sole trader or partner than as a company director, which gives you greater scope for making a claim.

The second point to bear in mind here is that for an unincorporated trader, business and personal tax are one and the same. This means that every penny of tax saved has a direct effect on the income available to you.

1.3. THE TAX RULES

1.3.1. Rule 1 - Incorporated business

The rules for limited companies follow the same principles as those for unincorporated businesses. Here, however, there is a fundamental difference: with sole traders and partnerships there is no distinction in law between the business and the person or people operating that business. This is why we arrive at a situation where private expenses are "added back" as described above.

With a limited company comes the "veil of incorporation", which has been used to describe the separation between the business owners (the shareholders) and the company itself. In the eyes of the law they are two separate entities.

What this means is that expenses invoiced to the company belong to the company itself and can be properly charged to the company. They do not belong to the directors who are running the company or the shareholders who own it. (NOTE. You can't just charge all your household expenses to the company because of the "wholly and exclusively" rule.)

1.3.2. Rule 2 - Unincorporated business

For an unincorporated business the costs charged have to be "wholly and exclusively for the purposes of the trade, profession or vocation". If not, you can't make a claim. What this means is that the expenditure must have been incurred because of your business and not merely that there was some incidental business element to it.

This is the "duality of purpose" rule which has been very rigidly applied by the courts in the past, and was interpreted very strictly in one ruling when a barrister was told that the dark clothing she wore in court could not be claimed as an expense because it served another purpose: the simple function of clothing. The fact that it served a secondary, professional purpose, was considered incidental.

Fortunately the Taxman is rarely as strict as this in his interpretation but it must be borne in mind that this is a long-established principle that he can turn to if pushed too hard.

What happens in practice is that any non-trade element of the expense is disallowed. This commonly comes in the form of an "add-back" for tax purposes, i.e. an adjustment made in the computations to mop up any private element, typically done on a percentage basis and often calculated after negotiation with the Taxman. It's often known as the "private use" adjustment.

1.3.3. Rule 3 - Benefits-in-kind

Any private element of a business expense is taxed on the employee under the benefits-in-kind system.

The most common examples are the free use of company cars and the provision of fuel, private medical insurance, and the payment of fees or subscriptions. Each year the employer will enter the value of the benefits on Form P11D and the employee will pay tax on those benefits, usually through an adjustment to their PAYE code.

1.3.4. Rule 4 - Employees

The third point is an extension of the "wholly and exclusively" rule and is applicable to employees, which of course includes company directors. The claimed expenditure must be "wholly, exclusively and necessarily incurred in the performance of the duties of the employment". Basically, if it's not necessary for the employee to incur the expense, then it can't be claimed.

This may, at first glance, look like a killer blow for anyone wanting to make a more "inventive" claim. Fortunately for us however, a company director's prime duty, as enshrined in company law, is to act in the best interests of the shareholders, i.e. to make a profit on their behalf. Therefore, any expenditure incurred to this end is a legitimate expense of the company. It will need to be demonstrated that this is the case should the Taxman make a challenge, but the point can be argued. Incur the expense for the business, even if there is an incidental private element, and it can properly be claimed.

1.3.5. Rule 5 - Dispensations

More good news for the employee/director is that there are times when a benefit does not need to be included on the P11D. This is when the Taxman gives a dispensation. This is basically an agreement that certain benefits do not need to be included on the P11D. He will only do this if he is satisfied that there will be no tax payable on the benefit.

An example of this is when an employee is paid travelling expenses. Strictly speaking these should normally be included on the P11D and then claimed back by the individual on his tax return. The net effect is that the benefit is cancelled out by the claim and everyone is happy. The dispensation means that there's no P11D for the company to fill in, and less paperwork for the Taxman to process.

1.4. SUMMARY

* Reduce taxable profits by converting some of your day-to-day personal expenditure into tax-deductible business expenses

* It doesn't matter that your accounting profit goes down; it's your spending power that counts

* The expenses have to be "wholly and exclusively" for the purposes of the trade: the expenditure must have been incurred because of your business

* An expense invoiced to the company is payable by the company; any private element is taxed as a benefit-in-kind

* Expenses claimed by an employee have to be "wholly, exclusively and necessarily incurred in the performance of their duties"

* Take advantage of the grey areas to get your tax bills reduced.

2. Claiming through your company

As we touched on in Chapter 1, there are two ways in which you can claim expenses through your company. The first is as an employee and the second is as a shareholder/director. We will look at each situation in turn.

We will also consider the situation in which the company pays the bill in the first place and what procedures should be followed in these circumstances.

2.1. HOW DO I CLAIM AS AN EMPLOYEE?

A company director is usually an employee of their company and therefore subject to the strict rules applied to earnings from employment. There are three ways by which an employee can obtain tax relief for expenses incurred on company business.

2.1.1. Claiming on your tax return

Any expense which you can incur as an employee can be claimed as a deduction from your earnings by entering the amount in boxes 1.32 - 1.35 on the employment pages of your personal tax return. This will reduce your taxable income and can often lead to a tax refund.

Advantages

- This is a simple and straightforward method with minimal paperwork

- Under self-assessment, the claim for deduction may never be challenged, particularly if it's one that's repeated from year to year.

Disadvantages

- Only the tax deducted is refunded, never the full expense. So if you incur expenses of £100 and pay tax at 40% you will only get £40 back. Similarly, a basic rate taxpayer will receive a refund of £22

- Although they can get through unchallenged, this is the exception not the rule, particularly for a new claim. For larger claims, the Taxman will almost certainly ask for further information before allowing them

- The rules for claiming a deduction as an employee, as we saw in Chapter 1, are very strict and have been interpreted very rigidly by the courts (remember the "wholly, exclusively and necessarily" rule)

- There is no deduction in the accounts of the company and therefore no reduction in the company's Corporation Tax liability.

2.1.2. Claiming a reimbursement

This is where the company refunds the full amount of the expense, or in the case of motor expenses, uses the approved mileage rates to make the reimbursement. The mechanics of this are more complicated than the simple process of a claim through your tax return and are best illustrated by way of an example.

Example

Jim, a company director, draws £100 per month from his company for entertaining business associates and potential customers. At the end of the tax year the company accountant adds up the receipts and vouchers supplied by Jim which are the actual costs of the entertaining. They total £1,100.

The company accountant will now make an entry on Jim's P11D for the year at Section N under the "Entertaining" heading as follows; "Cost to you £1,200"; "Amount made good £1,100"; "Taxable Amount £100". "Cost to you" means cost to the employer. "Amount made good" is the actual expenditure incurred on company business and "Taxable Amount" is the benefit-in-kind. Jim will now enter £100 in box 1.23 on the employment pages of his tax return and he will be taxed on this along with the rest of his earnings. However, if Jim had actually spent £1,300, he would normally claim the extra £100 from the company, and the P11D entries are; "Cost to you £1,300"; "Amount made good £1,300"; "Taxable payment £0".

If Jim didn't claim the additional £100 from the company he would enter the expense on his tax return. However, he would only be entitled to the tax deduction as discussed at 2.1.1. He will effectively be out of pocket by the difference.

Advantages

- The full amount of the expense incurred is obtained, not just the tax refund

- The company will often have an expense charged against profit in its accounts and therefore reduce its Corporation Tax liability (NOTE. This is never the case for entertaining customers, etc.)

- If done correctly, this method of completing the entries on form P11D and then the tax return gives greater legitimacy to the expense claim. There's nothing the Taxman likes more than correct procedures.

Disadvantages

- As with claiming on your tax return, the Taxman can still challenge the deduction under the "wholly, exclusively and necessarily" rule, even if every I is dotted and every T crossed

- There's more paperwork to complete: the company (which may well mean you or your accountant) will have to complete the entries on form P11D in addition to those already being entered on your tax return. The company will need records to back up the entries it makes on the P11D.

2.1.3. Claiming via a dispensation

A dispensation is an agreement with the Taxman that certain expense payments made do not need to be included on the P11D or on the tax return, the only proviso being that they attract a full tax deduction in the hands of the employee.

NOTE. In a nutshell, the amount being refunded to the employee exactly covers the amount you would be able to claim back on your tax return and therefore the Taxman isn't going to be out of pocket.

What can be covered

The Taxman's website says any type of expenses payments (apart from round sum allowances) and most benefits-in-kind can be covered, including:

- Qualifying travel expenses (but not business mileage payments because this is dealt with under special rules)

- Entertaining

- Subscriptions to professional bodies or learned societies.

A dispensation can also apply to non-cash vouchers and credit tokens provided to cover expenses.

What cannot be covered

Includes:

- Company cars and vans that are taxable

- Private medical insurance

- Cheap loans.

Conditions

The Taxman will only allow the dispensation if he is sure that:

- No tax would be payable by the employees on expenses paid or benefits provided

- Expenses claims are independently checked and authorised within the firm and, where possible, are supported by receipts.

This second condition presents us with a problem where the owner/manager of the business is the sole employee, or if the directors are effectively authorising their own expense claims. However, it's still possible to use the system if the expenses claimed are fully supported by documentation and your accountant regularly reviews a sample of them.

Change in circumstances

Because a dispensation can only cover the circumstances for which it was issued, and the type and amounts of expenses payments and benefits it specifically refers to, the Taxman will need to be informed of any changes for it to remain effective.

The example given on the Taxman's website is a modification of the system for controlling expenses payments or an alteration to the scale rates for expenses.

If the scale rates are amended in line with price changes, then the Taxman will normally agree without asking further questions, but any changes will mean that the dispensation should not be used until the Taxman has renewed his authorisation.

The only time the Taxman will remove his authorisation is when the situation for which the dispensation was given no longer applies. So in effect once the dispensation has been given, you can keep it until you no longer require it.

Advantages

- Unlike with certain benefits-in-kind, there's no NI due on payments made under a dispensation. This applies to both the company and the employee making the claim

- There are no entries to make on the tax return for the individual or on the P11D for the employer, so cutting down on the paperwork

- The expenses and benefits are not included as part of your tax assessment or PAYE codes.

Disadvantages

- The system is really designed for companies with a number of employees all making similar claims for similar expenses. If you're only going to be making one or two claims a year then you may decide it's not worth it

- Getting the Taxman's permission to use the system means that the chances of getting away with any "imaginative" claims are almost always nil.

2.2. HOW CAN I CLAIM AS A DIRECTOR/SHAREHOLDER?

2.2.1. Director's loan account

Being the owner as well as the manager of your business gives you an advantage not available to ordinary employees. This is because, as a general rule, it's you who runs the company and therefore it's you who ultimately decides what expenses the company incurs. As we outlined in Chapter 1, you can rent an upmarket address if you want to; whether it makes good business sense to do so is another matter, but the choice is still yours.

This is where you can use a bit of imagination and achieve what we looked at previously: getting your personal expenditure into the company as business expenses, and you can do this by utilising your Director's Loan Account (DLA).

NOTE. A DLA typically arises when a company is set up and the shareholders/directors put their own funds into the company as start-up capital. The company now owes this money to the directors and the funds are available to be drawn on as required, subject to the cash being available.

TIP. The DLA can also be used as a mechanism for the introduction of expenses to the company.

Example

Taking our example from earlier, Jim, who is a company director, has spent £1,300 of his own money on entertaining business customers. But because all of the company's spare cash is tied up in working capital, Jim decides not to draw the £1,300 from the company just yet. However, because he's spent the money on company business he knows he can add the sum to his DLA and charge the entertaining in the accounts. The £1,300 is now owed to Jim and he can claim it at a later date.

You could just as easily have waived the money; after all the company belongs to you, so it's only like paying yourself back from your own sources, isn't it? Wrong!

Example

Let's say we wind things on another year and we're into a new accounting period. The company now has surplus cash and Jim wants to pay himself a bonus so that he can take Mrs. Jim on a holiday that, by coincidence, just happens to cost £1,300. As we know, Jim can't just draw the cash from the company bank account without paying tax on the withdrawal. He has three options:

1. *Pay himself a bonus under PAYE*
2. *Pay himself a dividend*
3. *Borrow the money from the company.*

Each of the options will give rise to either a company or a personal tax bill, or in the case of Option 3, both. Option 3 also means the money has to be paid back, so we're back where we started.

Let's say Jim goes for Option 2 and the company declares a dividend of £1,300. As a higher-rate taxpayer, Jim will have to pay an extra £325 under self-assessment.

To take the concept one step further, let's imagine that Jim pays himself a salary under PAYE and each month he spends exactly what he takes home, with the result that he doesn't have the additional £325 to pay his personal tax bill. The result? He needs to pay himself another bonus from the company.

Tip. By putting an amount through your DLA as an expense you can simply withdraw the cash tax-free.

Documentation

As with everything to do with the Taxman, you must have adequate documentation to support your claim. So if it's an entertaining expense this means keeping receipts, bar bills, credit-card vouchers etc. This may seem like a chore but the more evidence you can gather, the stronger your case.

Note. However, there are no special rules to worry about here. The documentation kept in support of your claim forms part of the company's books in the same way as any other expense invoices do. Unlike putting an entry on your tax return or on a P11D, these claims are not separately identifiable from the rest of the company's day-to-day expenses which will eventually appear in the annual accounts.

This doesn't mean they won't ever be queried by the Taxman. They could be picked up and challenged through an enquiry into the company's tax return or on a PAYE control visit. The point is that the Taxman isn't put on notice that these claims are being made which increases their chances of getting "lost" in the accounts.

What can I claim through my DLA?

The simple answer is: anything and everything, so long as it meets the criteria set out in Chapter 1: it must have been "wholly and exclusively" incurred for the purposes of the trade (NOTE. The "necessarily" part doesn't apply here because it's an ordinary business expense not an employee expense).

So it's not just entertaining that you can claim for. It could be a "use of home" claim for doing the books on the kitchen table, calculated as a percentage of your household bills, or perhaps a mileage expense using the appropriate statutory rates.

Advantages

- It's simple and straightforward with no P11Ds or entries on your tax return to worry about

- You don't have to get prior approval from the Taxman to get the expense reimbursed

- There's no "necessarily" test to comply with

- You always get a full, tax-free reimbursement and it can be drawn as and when required

- The company gets a full deduction as appropriate.

Disadvantages

- You must have a certain amount of documentation to support your claim.

2.2.2. The company pays the bill

As we saw in Chapter 1, an invoice issued to the company is a legitimate company expense and is rightly payable by the company. It may not always be allowable for tax purposes or there may be some personal tax to pay because of the "wholly and exclusively" rule, but nevertheless this is one way in which a personal expenditure can become a business expense.

Home phone bill

A common example of this is the company paying the director's home phone bill. This is legitimised on the ground that many owner/managers make business calls in the evenings and at weekends. Added to this element of business use is the convenience of paying the bill on one account along with the office phone, fax, and Internet etc. Any private calls, plus the rental which is always classed as private, are taxed as a benefit-in-kind and will have to be declared on form P11D.

With something like the company paying a private phone bill it's difficult to tell where the business element starts and the private element finishes. Unlike with, say, a company car, there are no specific rules to follow when calculating the benefit. Strictly speaking, each call should be analysed between business and private, but this is not always practicable and as a result, a "reasonable" percentage is often agreed with the Taxman.

TIP. One important point to remember is that any invoice has to be issued in the name of the company at the company address, not the director at his home address. If this isn't done then it's treated as being remuneration and the whole bill becomes subject to NI.

WARNING. What you can't do is charge expenses falsely to the company; it's one thing having an expense with a private element; it's another thing altogether to have purely personal bills invoiced to the company. This is known as the "pecuniary liability principle", where the employer effectively discharges a debt between the director and a third party, and it will be treated as earnings by the Taxman.

Advantages

- The Taxman will often agree the private element on a percentage basis so there's not much record-keeping to do
- A bill in the company's name gives it extra credibility
- There's no having to claim an expense as it's already been paid for you.

Disadvantages

- You have to include the private element on a P11D.

2.3. WHAT ARE THE KEY THINGS TO REMEMBER?

Claiming expenses through your limited company can be done in a variety of ways, and the particular method you use may well vary depending on the nature of the expense. But the most important points to remember are:

- If you claim a deduction on your tax return you can only ever get tax relief at a maximum of 40%; never the whole amount back

- For every pound you can get out of the company you will be saving the equivalent in salary plus the income tax and NI that would have been due under PAYE

- Make sure your paperwork's in order so that you can support any claim if there's a challenge. It doesn't just make life easier but gives the Taxman more confidence that the claim is legitimate.

3. Unincorporated businesses

This chapter looks at how to claim expenses if you're self-employed, either as a sole trader or in a partnership, or if you've got some part-time freelance work as well as your main employment.

The main difference between a limited company and an unincorporated business is that with a company the owners are protected from their creditors by their limited liability status, whereas a sole trader or partner doesn't enjoy this protection. There is no separation in the eyes of the law between personal and business debts.

Whilst this can have obvious disadvantages, the unincorporated business has a distinct advantage over its limited company counterpart, and that is the comparative ease with which expenses can be claimed.

This is not to say it's easier for an expense to qualify as allowable for tax purposes; they still have to pass the "wholly and exclusively" test before the Taxman will let them get through. What is does mean though, is that there are far fewer formalities to go through before the expense will see it's way into the business accounts. There are no special forms to fill in, like the P11D, or formal agreements like the dispensation, both of which can put the Inspector on the lookout.

As the owner/manager of an unincorporated business, the amount of tax you pay is not related to the income you draw from your business but from the profit it makes. This is an important point to bear in mind when considering what extra expenses you can claim through your business, and you should always follow this simple rule of thumb: there's no point claiming if there's no tax advantage.

Example

Take entertaining as an example. In Chapter 2 we looked at Jim who could gain an advantage from claiming his entertaining expenses as a reimbursement from his company. That's fine for him because as a director on PAYE he's saving himself and his company the tax and NI on the extra salary he would have to draw to make up the difference.

Let's say that Jim has a brother, John, and he's the proprietor of an unincorporated business. Like Jim, John spends about £100 each month on entertaining customers. Now if John claims a refund of these expenses from his business bank account he would only be drawing money out of his business to pay himself. Yes the expense would hit the

Profit & Loss account, but because entertaining customers is always disallowed for tax purposes it would simply be added back to profits and John would be back at square one.

If, on the other hand, he's converted the spare bedroom at home and turned it into his office, or he makes a lot of business calls in the evenings on his home phone, then all the costs associated with these can be claimed through his firm's books.

3.1. HOW CAN I MAKE A CLAIM?

3.1.1. Claiming on your tax return

The way you make an expense claim is to enter the right accounting information on the Self-Employed or Partnership pages of your self-assessment tax return. The Taxman will then transfer the data from your return to his computer to calculate your tax bill.

So, to get an appropriate tax deduction, you have to get the expense into your accounts and here we will look at the ways you can achieve this.

3.1.2. Claiming a reimbursement

This is where your business simply refunds any amount paid by you for a business expense.

Example

Let's say you're doing the weekly shopping in the local supermarket and they're selling personal computers at a one-off, bargain price. What's more, the spec is exactly right to replace the now obsolete machine back at the office. A chance like this is too good to miss and so you pay for it with your personal credit card.

To get the computer onto the business books you can now write a cheque from the business account for the full cost of the computer and pay it into your personal account and you're all square. You will then have to reference the cheque payment in the business books to the invoice for the PC. This way you will be able to distinguish it from personal drawings and the appropriate tax relief can be claimed.

Advantages

The advantages of making a reimbursement in this way are firstly that it gives a complete record of the transaction and helps to reduce the overlap between business and personal expenses. This is particularly important when it comes to preparing the year-end accounts because; **(1)** you don't miss making the claim; and **(2)** it's often difficult to remember what you made payments for with the passage of time. Referencing it to the invoice will give you all the information you need.

Completeness of your records is also important when it comes to a visit from the Taxman or VATman. If he can see at first glance exactly what's going on it puts him in the comfort zone he likes that only comes with a nicely kept set of books. The more comfortable he is the sooner he will leave you alone.

3.1.3. Claiming via an invoice

What we're considering here is the situation where your expenses are paid along with all the other costs of running the business, but in particular where the expense has a mixed business/private element.

> *Example*
>
> *An obvious example is the petrol account at the local garage where you fill up once a week and the account is made out to the firm. Unless you never take the vehicles home there will always be some private use associated with the expense.*

As we saw in the Chapter 1, the private element of a business expense is dealt with by making a "Private Use" adjustment, usually done on a percentage basis. The appropriate amount is then added back to your profits so that only the business element of the expense gets tax relief.

Naturally, you will want the private proportion to be as low as possible, while the Taxman will want the exact opposite. But at what point does a private expense that has a business element switch to being a business expense with some private use?

By getting bills with a mixed use invoiced to the firm at its business address, you'll provide most of the evidence to satisfy an enquiring Taxman. We're not suggesting fraudulent claims here; there has to be a genuine business element, and one that is not merely "incidental" to the expense. You still have to calculate a private percentage that he can agree to but by presenting the bill in this light you're approaching it from the angle of "business with private use" rather than the other way around.

> *Example*
>
> *A good example of this is the home telephone bill that gets paid with the firm's own bill. The justification for doing this is that you make calls in the evening and at weekends, and it's administratively more convenient to pay all the bills on one account. There will now be an increase in*

the private use add-back but there will be an increase in the tax relief claimed too.

3.1.4. Claiming it as capital introduced

The term "capital introduced" is usually associated with cash put into a business as start-up capital, or perhaps an injection of funds from your own sources to help with cash-flow. But the term can also be used to describe any payment of cash or the transfer of an asset into the business by you, no matter how big or small. Its relevance to us in the context of claiming business expenses can best be illustrated by an example.

Example

Let's say that after John's first year of trading the business profits are £10,000. He always does his bookkeeping at home and by the end of the year calculates that the extra household expenses incurred doing this comes to £1,000. He will need to get this additional expense into his books to be able to claim tax relief.

He could simply write himself a cheque for that amount and reference it to his calculations. He could try getting the bills invoiced to the company in the first place, but he would have a job convincing the Taxman that the business element was not merely incidental. The third way of getting an expense into the business books is by making an adjustment through the Capital Account. The Capital Account is the balance on the books after all the assets have been added up and all the liabilities deducted.

The Capital Account can be increased by the owners of the business adding capital, and decreased by making drawings (effectively payments to themselves) from it. The other way that the Capital Account is increased is by earning profits, while losses will have the opposite effect.

John can reduce his profits by making a book entry to both his expenses (a debit) of £1,000 under the heading of "Use of Home as Office". A corresponding entry to his capital account (a credit) of the same amount will be described as "Capital Introduced". This way the books will still balance and the extra tax relief can be claimed. The capital account balance will be exactly as it was before because the credit to the account of £1,000 expenses is balanced out by the £1,000 reduction in profit for the year.

The effect would be the same if John had written a cheque from his personal account and paid it into his business account (the "Capital Introduced" bit), and then taken the £1,000 and spent it on renting office space.

Advantage

- The advantage of taking this approach is that it's simple to do. There's no formal paperwork and no cheques to write. All you have to do is have sufficient documentation to back up your claim, such as paid bills and calculations, if you're making an apportionment.

Disadvantages

- A downside to making adjustments to your Capital Account relates to your tax return. This is because box 3.113 of the accounting information pages (of both the individual and the partnership tax return) is specifically for the amount of Capital Introduced. This means that the Taxman can home straight in on entries in this box, and if he doesn't like the look of them he can start to ask questions

- Another disadvantage is that in certain situations it's difficult to claim the VAT back on the expense.

3.2. WHAT DOCUMENTATION DO I NEED?

Generally speaking, there are no hard and fast rules dictating exactly what records your business should keep and you are allowed to organise your records to suit your own needs. Much will depend on the complexity of your business, your own preferences and the abilities of the bookkeeper. The Taxman acknowledges that businesses keep a variety of records ranging from a simple collection of copy invoices and receipts for purchases, through to a fully computerised bookkeeping system.

The basic rule is that the record kept must back up the claim. The best form of documentation will always be an invoice for the expense issued to the business. However, the Taxman will accept things like a cheque stub backed up by a bank statement, or an informal receipt that records the basic information of supplier, date and amount paid.

Keep as much information as you can to support your claim for the apportionment of an expense, particularly if the private element is small. Again, there are no particular rules on this, and the Taxman's website is silent on how he approaches the subject. In fact, certain sections of his rulebook have been kept hidden from the general public, meaning he either doesn't want us to know his views or he doesn't want us to know he has no idea what's reasonable and what isn't.

- Having your trading name and address on an invoice or other document will always help your claim

- A description of your working practices is always useful; this will give the Taxman a better understanding of how you operate and how the expense relates to your operation

- If the claim is unusual, be ready to explain why it relates to your business and what benefits you derived from it. If you booked a night in an expensive hotel tell him about the business meeting you had the next day: where it was held, who was there, what the agenda was. (You don't have to mention that your favourite West End show happened to be on that evening.)

3.3. CAN I CLAIM THE VAT?

The most important thing to remember when claiming VAT back on a purchase, is that you must have a valid VAT invoice to make the claim. This is true whether there is private use or not.

3.3.1. Claims through your Capital Account

It can be almost impossible to claim the VAT back on an expense calculated and claimed through your Capital Account. This is true for an expense such as a "Use of Home" calculation, because any extra cost you incur such as heating and lighting will be made out to you, an individual, not your VAT-registered business. (NOTE. Because you're not getting the VAT back on these, don't forget to base your calculations on a gross, not net of VAT, basis.)

However, it would not be true for a computer purchased as an individual, but used by the business. It would be perfectly acceptable to the VATman if you claimed the VAT back on this purchase even if you introduced this asset to your business through your capital account.

3.3.2. Claiming a proportion of the VAT

If you purchase goods or services which have some business and non-business use, only the business proportion of the input VAT can be reclaimed from the VATman. There are two ways you can do this; **(1)** you carry out a one-off apportionment of the VAT; or **(2)** reclaim all the VAT, and then account for the cost of using the goods for private purposes in each tax period by adding this to your output tax, i.e. making the non-business element part of your sales VAT. The result is the same either way.

3.3.3. Using a scale rate for motor expenses

The cost of running a vehicle, as far as the recovery of input tax is concerned, is divided between fuel costs and all other running expenses. With fuel, as with general goods and services, you can only claim VAT back on the business use. Again there are two choices; **(1)** you apportion the VAT between business and private use; or **(2)** you can apply the fuel scale charge to the VAT. Either way, you need to keep invoices to support your claim.

With repairs and servicing, the rules are more generous. Basically, you can claim back any VAT you're charged if the business paid for the work, even if there's private motoring or you don't reclaim VAT on the fuel.

3.4. WHAT ARE THE KEY POINTS TO REMEMBER?

- The amount you pay yourself, as the owner of an unincorporated business, doesn't affect your tax bill. To reduce the amount you pay, you must have tax-deductible expenses

- To get tax relief, the expense has to get on to your tax return through your year-end accounts

- The three main ways of achieving this are; **(1)** a reimbursement to you, backed up by appropriate documentation; **(2)** your business also settles your part of a joint bill, which has been invoiced to it; and **(3)** accounting adjustments through your capital account, again backed up by paperwork

- The amount and quality of the documentation you keep in support of your claim can be crucial; if you haven't got an invoice, don't worry, the Taxman will often accept more informal paperwork

- If challenged, give the Taxman as much information about your business and the circumstances of the claim as possible

- What is precisely business and what is private is still a grey area and can only be agreed on a case-by-case basis, so it's worth arguing with a stubborn Taxman

- When claiming VAT back, you must always have a valid VAT invoice

- You should apportion the VAT you're reclaiming between business and private, and only claim the business amount

- With motor expenses you can apportion VAT on your fuel costs or use the fuel scale charge. All the VAT on repairs and servicing is reclaimable.

4. Dealing with the Taxman

As with all tax planning you need to be one step ahead of the Taxman. This includes having documentation to hand to take care of the awkward Inspector that everybody comes across from time to time.

In truth, the tax rules for deduction of expenses are so strict that they are normally allowed because the Taxman eventually takes a reasonable view. This is very important to know because it will affect the way you approach him. As a general rule, courtesy and a professional approach pay dividends because negotiations will invariably be required over expenses.

NOTE. Chapter 30 also provides a resource for dealing with the Taxman, with relevant case law, useful websites, where to find the official guidance, etc.

4.1. HOW WILL THE TAXMAN KNOW?

With your company's annual self-assessment tax return (CT600) you have to file a full set of accounts, including a detailed profit and loss account. Selecting an expense heading from this, that has perhaps increased dramatically compared to last year, the Taxman may ask for more details/analysis (as an aspect enquiry) thus revealing the costs to the company of a personal expense.

Example

If your company can buy medical insurance cover more cheaply than you can, it may make sense for your company to meet this expense. What if your company forgets to put this on your P11D?

If you have booked this cost to say "Insurances" and the Taxman asks for an analysis of this expense heading during an enquiry into your company, he will look for corresponding disclosure of medical insurance on your P11D. If it's not there your company has submitted an incorrect return and you are into his penalty regime as well as having to pay employers' NI on the figure and interest for late payment.

He will go as far as to send a note to the Inspector who deals with your income tax return to say that he thinks it's incomplete too. Oops!

4.2. HOW SHOULD I REACT?

How should you handle the Taxman if he comes knocking on your door asking for details about your expenses? In fact, how do you mount a successful defence against the implied suggestion that you might simply be "trying it on"?

Remember, the Taxman doesn't have all the answers. His job is to make sure you're not underpaying your taxes, and he has a big book of rules to help him. But there are also rules in place to see that he plays fair, and there are people looking over his shoulder to make sure he's not wasting time chasing small amounts of tax. If it's seen as uneconomic to pursue an argument then he will try to reach a compromise. At the end of the day, tax law is full of grey areas and as we have seen it's not always possible to demonstrate clearly where "business" begins and "personal" ends.

There are two golden rules to follow here; **(1)** it's a paper audit. If you've got the documentation right any argument with the Taxman will be halfway won before you even start; and **(2)** don't be intimidated into backing down without a fight.

4.2.1. Does he always ask the same questions?

The Taxman's procedures during enquiries generally run along the same lines. He will make a list of all the areas he has a problem with and will write to you asking for information. If you have a tax advisor they will be sent copies of all correspondence. Here are the dos and don'ts in response to this:

- Never ignore him. If there are penalties, the rate charged will be reduced if he thinks you've been co-operative. Write a brief letter acknowledging his enquiry and that you will answer in full in due course. This will give you time to prepare your defence

- Gather as much information backing up your claim as you can. If you haven't got documentation, write down the facts behind the claim. For example, if you had a trip abroad you need to demonstrate how it helped your business and that it wasn't just a holiday

- Write your reply, responding to each point in turn. Keep to the facts, giving him as much as he needs but no more. Include supporting documentation if you have it

- Ask yourself some questions: why is he asking for this? Is he entitled to it? Is it relevant to his enquiry?

- If he has any technical queries, get a tax advisor if you haven't already appointed one.

The Taxman will then consider your response, and either write back for further details or come up with a figure he wants to assess you on.

4.2.2. Will I need to attend an interview?

Generally speaking a meeting with the Taxman is not required, particularly if there are only a small number of queries that are relatively straightforward.

4.3. WHOLLY AND EXCLUSIVELY ATTACK

The Taxman will want to disallow expenses if they are not "wholly and exclusively" for the company's trade.

Let's say you've incurred some expenses partly for business and partly for personal reasons. The rule is that the expenses must be wholly and exclusively incurred for the purposes of the business. This leads to the most important principle, which is duality of purpose. What this means is that if you incur some expense partly for business reasons and partly for other reasons you don't get part of your expenses allowed - you will get none of them.

Example

The best example of a duality of purpose case was that of Miss Anne Mallalieu, a barrister who was obviously able to argue her case with great skill. She still lost. She claimed the expense of buying and keeping clean the black clothing that she was required to wear in court. She did not like the black clothing and wore it only for work. What the Taxman successfully claimed was that she did not only buy the clothes for wearing in court - she had another purpose which was she needed to wear clothes to remain decent. The latter purpose was not a business purpose and therefore she infringed the duality of purpose rule.

Fortunately, the Taxman is rarely as strict as this in his approach and often allows expenses where they have a clear business purpose - providing there is no other purpose which is obvious. But watch out - if you press too hard you must remember that at the end of the day the Taxman could simply say the magic words "duality of purpose" and your claim will be blocked.

Don't be led into making general statements which indicate dual purpose for any expenditure. Provided the primary purpose of the expenditure was wholly and exclusively business, it does not matter that you derive some personal benefit from it - that will not preclude a tax deduction.

What matters is that the expenditure was not incurred for the purpose of getting the private benefit as well.

Example

If you have to go to France during the summer to see a client or otherwise for a bona fide business purpose you may as well enjoy yourself in your spare time. This does not matter providing this was not one of the reasons for going. It was just a fortuitous and pleasant side effect. During an investigation don't be drawn into admitting that you thought it would be a good place to have a good time as well, because this will prejudice your tax deduction.

Rule of thumb. If the personal benefit is just a fortuitous and pleasant side effect of an otherwise bona fide business expense your "dual purpose" expenses will be allowed for tax. Don't be misled into saying otherwise.

4.4. CLAIMING IT'S PART OF YOUR REMUNERATION

In order to manage the business, a company has to attract and retain key employees. The cost of this usually meets the wholly and exclusively test, provided it's not excessive for the duties performed. Therefore, if you reassess your remuneration package (as an employee) to include in it a particular expense you would like the company to incur (as a benefit-in-kind for yourself) this is, in our opinion, wholly and exclusively for the purposes of the trade.

Company law. Remember, directors' remuneration is determined by the shareholders at their Annual General Meeting. If the shareholders can't decide what is necessary for the company's trade, who can, Mr Taxman?

However, if challenged on this "part of your remuneration" argument by the Taxman, you'll need to be able to provide him with a copy of what was agreed in writing between you and your company - both amongst the company board minutes (see 4.6) and as an addition to your contract of employment.

Example

Amendment to contract of employment
As from November 30, 2006, the company will contract and pay for the painting and decorating of two rooms in your principal private residence each year. This benefit-in-kind is from that date part of your remuneration package with the company and will be provided by it subject to the company having sufficient funds to do so.

Further, if you've gone to the trouble of getting you and your company's paperwork right, so that a company expense can be legitimately treated as a benefit-in-kind, make sure it also appears on your P11D. Otherwise the Taxman can start arguing that it's earnings and tax it more heavily.

4.5. NATIONAL MINIMUM WAGE

The remuneration defence against a wholly and exclusively attack relies on you actually having a contract of employment with your company. You might not have one at present because to do so automatically brings you within the National Minimum Wage (NMW) requirements and hence incur a small tax bill.

Example

In 2006/7 you've planned to take £5,035 (the tax and NI-free amount) by way of salary from your company and the rest of what you need by way of dividends. This is less than the NMW for an adult working 35 hours a week for 48 weeks of the year, which works out at £8,484 (35 x 48 x £5.05). The income tax bill on this level of salary works out as:

TOTAL SALARY **£8,484**	TAX RATE	£
On first £5,035	0%	0.00
On next £2,150	10%	215.00
On balance of £1,299	22%	285.78
Total income tax bill		**500.78**
Employees' NI (£8,484 - £5,035 = £3,449)	11%	379.39
Employers' NI (on £3,449)	12.8%	441.47
Total NI cost		**820.86**
Extra tax cost of NMW salary		1,321.64
Less Corporation Tax deduction on extra salary plus employer' NI (£3,449 + £441.47= £3,890.47)	19%	(739.19)
Net tax cost of extra salary		**582.45**

NOTE. The NMW for an adult increases to £5.35 per hour from October 1, 2006.

In our opinion, for a small additional tax cost (in our example £600) of complying with the NMW you can get thousands of pounds of personal expenses classed as tax deductible in the company, under the banner of it being an agreed and documented addition to your contract of employment.

4.6. EXPENSE CLAIMS

Expenses that straddle the border between business and personal pose the highest enquiry risk. Examples include: travel, meals, entertainment, business mileage, home offices, insurance, and phone costs. These are examined by the Taxman in every full enquiry, since he suspects you are deducting personal costs, however, unfair that appears to you and us.

One simple key to protecting these deductions is to first highlight any special record-keeping requirements for these expenses. This can provide an opportunity for making your return enquiry-proof - even for items well into the grey area between business and personal.

When the Taxman's manuals set specific paperwork requirements for a deduction and you meet them, a tax Inspector normally has little real incentive to enquire further - and a real incentive not to, since they are under pressure to close cases and collect more tax as soon as possible.

Example

If your records for meals show, if relevant, whom you entertained, when, where, the business purpose and the amount, then an Inspector is very unlikely to insist on verification that you really discussed business at the meal. To do so wouldn't be cost-effective and would add to the backlog of cases - so with this level of record keeping you can expect the deduction to be allowed. Virtually enquiry proof.

If the Taxman starts off examining records that are full and complete, then moves on to other items that are less than perfect examples (but still professionally presented), he is likely to review the latter in a manner that still leads to a satisfactory enquiry result because:

Reason 1. The overall quality of the records indicates that you aren't trying to "get away with something", so suspicions are not aroused.

Reason 2. High quality records increase your chance of success at an appeal, should you go there. The Taxman knows this and so has a practical reason to give enough to avoid an appeal (see 4.9.).

Reason 3. When you present records in good order, you are being considerate, helping the Taxman to do his job - and it's human nature for consideration to be returned, as well as allowing penalties to be reduced.

However, there are two easy ways to lose the enquiry-proofing that good records can give to grey area deductions;

(1) No matter how complete your records are, the Taxman is going to have a hard time believing deductions which push the rules too far. For example, claiming three meals a day, business mileage seven days a week and work expenses for 52 weeks a year. These only invite questions about your honesty that good records are meant to prevent. So claim less than the full whack, e.g. a claim for 48 weeks allows for holidays.

(2) Another way to make excellent records worthless, is to show the Taxman that they might be false. For example, car maintenance records often snag those who exaggerate business mileage records in their diaries. So make sure you don't get caught out by this.

It's worth spending the time now annotating your expense claims as to their business purpose. Then you can direct the Taxman to your best documented deductions first and hopefully reduce the risk of a detailed enquiry.

4.7. BOARD MINUTES

Some time in the future the Taxman may enquire into your company's expenses. If so, he likes to put his own spin on your innocent actions. But there is something you can do now with your company's board minutes that will later stop him in his tracks.

You make many decisions, any one of which could have tax implications. If you are investigated and the Taxman thinks he can collect more tax he will say that the decision you made was for the "purpose of avoiding tax". But if you can show otherwise, the law is on your side, and this only takes a minute.

He may try, but the Taxman has no right to tell you how to run your business. He can apply tax law but he will have trouble making it stick in borderline areas if you can show how the expenditure was intended to benefit the business.

Rule of thumb. Generally, any note of, for example, a telephone call or a meeting, made at the time or shortly afterwards can be produced in court as evidence in a dispute. A note made at the time shows what you were thinking - your intentions were good.

The directors of a company may have to consult each other, albeit informally. But some of these meetings have to be on a formal basis so that decisions taken are recorded as board minutes - which then form a statutory record. Boring, but necessary for company law purposes.

Most company minute books are on a shelf somewhere gathering dust. All they usually contain are a few pages of annual meetings, share allotments and directors' appointments. But they can be used to record other matters such as the leasing or purchase of premises and agreement to loans/and or bank overdrafts. In practice these things are considered before the meeting and are only put to the board for approval. So all that gets recorded is the decision. But this can be used to stay one step ahead of the Taxman.

Example

A board minute could include a commercial reason for the company agreeing to add decorating arrangements to your remuneration package with the company. It might read as follows: "In recognition of your contribution to the company and to avoid you spending time away from company business at key times to undertake DIY, the company has decided that as part of your remuneration package it will contract and pay for the painting and decorating of two rooms in your principal private residence each year. This is, of course, subject to the company having sufficient funds to do so."

TIP. You can spike the Taxman's guns by recording your good intentions in a board minute at the time you make your decision. In cases where you think there may be a problem, post the signed minutes to the board members' home addresses. Keep yours and the envelope it came in to prove it was done at the time.

To charge penalties, the Taxman needs to show you were negligent in your tax affairs. A timely minute can make that charge of negligence difficult to sustain.

For the avoidance of doubt record your intentions in a board minute now. If, down the line, the Taxman wants to put another spin on things you've put up a stop sign. This way you stay one step ahead of him.

4.8. VALUING AN EXPENSE/BENEFIT-IN-KIND

If you want an expense to be taxed as a benefit-in-kind instead, then the contract with the supplier of the goods/services needs to be negotiated by, addressed to and be clearly a liability of the company (not yours). Otherwise the company is settling one of your liabilities and this can be reclassed by the Taxman as earnings with extra tax and NI to pay.

Where there is a benefit-in-kind, the taxable value is the "cost" the company incurs to provide the benefit rather than the market value of the goods/services.

TIP. Don't engineer a pre-set figure or just estimate based on a few facts. This will leave you open to a benefit figure being imposed by the Taxman and in the absence of other facts he may just use a price that pushes up the value of the benefit.

However, based on a tax case, you can use marginal cost to your company rather than a wholesale price or full cost. This means that you use just the additional cost of providing you with the benefit. For example, this would be the cost of purchasing the goods, plus any costs that vary in accordance with the quantity of goods purchased, for example, delivery charges, etc. However, you don't need to take account of fixed costs, such as rent etc.

Remember. There are, of course, no benefits to be entered for those employees earning less than £8,500 pa.

4.9. THREATEN HIM WITH THE COMMISSIONERS

If the Taxman doesn't accept your arguments about expenses and you think you have a good case, you can threaten to take this before the General Commissioners. This will test how strong a case the Taxman thinks he has.

But first write to the Taxman and ask him why he thinks he can take this contrary view. If nothing comes of this after 28 days, then write a letter to the District Inspector requesting that he review your case. It may be that a more experienced pair of eyes sees that a common sense approach is needed.

Again if nothing happens, then push the Taxman to focus on the facts by asking for a general hearing before a tax tribunal (the General Commissioners). In the same letter, send him a draft statement of agreed facts and documentation for agreement prior to that hearing. (The costs of an appeal to a tax tribunal are likely to be prohibitive so only use this tactic to get him to move from his incorrect position.)

As a compromise before actually going to the Commissioners, you could ask for the enquiry to be closed at a figure somewhere between his and yours. If he refuses ask for a "closure review" by another officer. If this doesn't get you the figure you want you then have to decide whether you actually do get the Commissioners involved.

4.10. WHAT IF I JUST HIDE IT AND HOPE?

4.10.1. What is hide it and hope?

For the high-risk takers there is an alternative approach, and that's the simple "hide it and hope" option. What this entails is putting purely personal expenses through the business in the hope that they stay hidden, and tackling the Taxman as and when he comes looking.

4.10.2. What are the penalties if discovered?

This is potentially an expensive strategy. Not only could it leave you with a nasty tax bill, it could also give rise to what the Taxman calls "culpable penalties", which is basically a fine for not getting things right in the first place. It can be charged at anything from 5% to 50% of the tax under-declared depending on how serious he thinks the offence is.

4.10.3. Will I be interviewed by the Taxman?

Generally speaking a meeting with the Taxman is not required. However, where you've gone down the route of "hide it and hope" with personal expenses, the chances of being called for one increases once you've been discovered. The important rules to remember with interviews are:

- Consider having the meeting at your premises: being on familiar territory can give you a big advantage

- Be co-operative: any penalties could be reduced as a result

- Rehearse your responses. That way he's less likely to trick you into saying the wrong thing

- Give full explanations but be concise. If you tell him too much it could open up further questions.

Remember, the Taxman's a civil servant, not a crown barrister or MI5 agent. He may be more experienced in these matters but he can only make a judgement on the information he has in front of him. Only you know the real facts; don't let him try to convince you otherwise.

4.10.4. Can the Taxman look at other years?

If the Taxman finds problems in one year he's going to assume the same thing applied in the past. But don't just let him widen his enquiry into earlier years. Ask him why he wants this information and under what authority he's asking for it: remember, the Taxman has strict rules to follow, he can't just go marching in to your premises and make unreasonable demands.

4.10.5. When do I negotiate?

Negotiation needs to be done before a Taxman's enquiry is closed and payment is being sought. What you need is a counter-argument, e.g. expenses or capital allowances that you didn't claim before, which may come to light if you go through your records in as much detail as he does.

TIP. With the Taxman, you have to negotiate when the enquiry is still open not when it's time to pay.

4.10.6. How will I know if the enquiry is finished?

When he's made his enquiries and you've answered his questions, get him to close the case as quickly as possible. There's no point in you running up extra interest costs for his convenience. Once the final bill comes, check his calculations to make sure they tally to the figures you supplied.

If there are penalties, remember that there's a discretionary element to this and it's possible to negotiate them down. Point out that you've been co-operative and that any errors were genuine mistakes.

Once the amount of tax due has been transferred to the Collector of Taxes (now called Receivables Managers), the stated policy is now "pay up or else". So expect requests for time to pay/paying by instalments to be met with comments like "well can't you borrow the money from someone else?". Don't be bullied, push for instalments and the official rate of interest on overdue amounts.

4.11. KEY POINTS

- The Taxman will want to disallow expenses if they are not "wholly and exclusively" for the benefit of the trade

- Provided the primary purpose of the expense was wholly and exclusively business, it doesn't matter that you derive some personal benefit from it

- Reassess your remuneration package to include in it a particular expense you would like the company to incur

- You might need a contract of employment with your company. To do so brings you within the National Minimum Wage (NMW) requirements

- Any note of a meeting made at the time or shortly afterwards can be produced as evidence in a dispute.

- Don't give in to all his demands without question. Check his results to see that they agree with the facts

- If the Taxman doesn't accept your arguments about expenses and you think you have a good case, you can threaten to take this before the General Commissioners. This will test how strong a case the Taxman thinks he has.

5. Use of home by a company

5.1. THE EXPENSE

Taking things home to work on or even making that important conference call at home needs somewhere you can shut yourself away from the rest of the household. When it's company business could the company pay you a flat rate for this "use of home as office"?

The standard tax treatment for any such payment would be for the company to claim a deduction for it, but then to put it on your annual return of benefits and expenses (P11D). Like all entries from the P11D, this has to go on the employment page of your self-assessment tax return as income for you. But then you put down the same figure on the next page as an "expense incurred in doing your job" - hence claiming a tax deduction. Income (P11D) now matches expenditure (claim) giving zero tax bills. However, your claim for expenses incurred when working at home might not be worth the ink used as it's almost impossible in practice to get it past the Taxman as being "necessary".

£2 a week for additional costs

Instead, where there is a formalised agreement to work at home, the first £2 a week of any payment will be tax and NI-free in all cases. Higher payments may also be tax-free where evidence can be provided by you of the additional expense incurred in carrying out your duties from home. NOTE. There is no wholly, exclusive and necessary condition here.

Renting alternative

A more lucrative alternative would be to get the payment from your company treated as rent instead of expenses. The company will get a tax deduction for the rent paid (provided it's not excessive) and if the rental income equals your own costs you will have a zero tax bill again.

What you're then left with is simply deciding what expenses are properly attributable to the provision of (furnished) accommodation to your company. The total of these is then used to set the level of rent received from the company. You can charge your company as little rent as you wish for using your property; it does not have to be at market value but it must not exceed it.

Expenses would include an appropriate proportion of heating and lighting costs, maintenance and repair costs and a proportion of mortgage interest, plus any expenses you incur at your company's specific request.

TIP. Agree a rental figure with the company from time to time based on the actual use made by making the accommodation available.

Back up this rental income assertion with a formal rent or licence agreement between you and the company and the property owners, i.e. you (and your spouse if owned jointly). This doesn't need to be a complicated document but does need to specify what has been agreed.

TIP. The rent you can negotiate is higher if use of the accommodation is extended to cover board meetings held at your home, particularly if there is no space at the office to do so. If the meeting starts at say 3pm and goes on into the evening and you provide dinner, the company can be asked to pay for that as well.

Non-domestic use

Could business rates be due on this non-domestic use of part of your home? The current consensus is that provided you are not being visited by clients, then this is not a problem. However, in order to prevent the loss of principal private residence relief on this part of your home when you sell it, use it for private as well as business purposes, e.g. keep the exercise bike or guest bed in the room.

TIP. To avoid any "exclusively-used for business" challenge, state in the rental agreement that the facilities are only let to the company for designated hours each week, for example, 9.00am to 5.00pm, Monday to Friday.

5.2. WHAT ARE THE POTENTIAL TAX SAVINGS?

Paying £2 a week for additional costs means another £104 tax and NI-free a year that your company can pay you.

If the company pays you, for example, an additional flat rate of £50 a week (£2,600 pa) for use of home as office, but the Taxman wants to treat this as additional net salary, you could end up paying additional income tax and employers' NI of £1,807 (£2,600/59 x 41), as a higher rate taxpayer.

If you can get the £50 treated as rent but matched with £50 worth of expenses, there will be no tax to pay.

5.3. THE PAPERWORK

By taking the following steps you will be making sure that there is no room for a challenge by the Taxman. And with all the paperwork done correctly there should be no risk of penalties arising at a later date either.

5.3.1. The board minute

Remember, any expense charged in the company's accounts has to meet the "wholly and exclusively" test that we talked about earlier. Getting a formal board minute drawn up demonstrates to the Taxman that the benefit was agreed by the company as a way of rewarding you for your services.

There is no need for any special wording, just a statement of the facts as a record for future reference.

> *Example*
>
> *"Meeting of the Board of Directors of XYZ Limited on .... at ....*
>
> *It was resolved that the company will pay rent to .... for office facilities at .... [address]. The rate to be reviewed annually under the terms and conditions of a formal licence agreement.*
>
> *Signed .... company secretary."*

5.3.2. Rental agreement

Back up this payment for office facilities with a licence agreement between you and your company setting out formal terms and conditions.

5.3.3. On the VAT return

There's no VAT involved in this expense.

5.3.4. On your P11D

No entry required.

5.3.5. In the company's accounts

Although there are no special disclosure requirements, if you include the payment for rent under "rent and rates" it reinforces your position that it's a business expense.

5.3.6. On your tax return

You'll need to record the rent you receive from your company as rental income on your tax return. Remember to claim the costs of supplying this facility to your company (in line with any specific requirements it might have).

5.4. LOW, MEDIUM AND HIGH-RISK STRATEGIES

5.4.1. Low-risk

Getting the paperwork right as described above cuts all risk down to an absolute minimum.

5.4.2. Medium-risk

If it's unclear that the payment is rent there's a risk that it will be treated as net salary and the Taxman will come looking for tax and NI on the gross equivalent.

5.4.3. High-risk

You pay yourself a round sum allowance from the company for the use of your home as an office. If discovered, the Taxman will want to treat this as net salary that needs grossing-up for unpaid tax and NI, plus interest and penalties to boot.

6. Garden maintenance

6.1. THE EXPENSE

You've heard from a colleague that they get their gardening paid for by the company. The Taxman is particular about private expenditure but you know there must be grey areas. Is this one?

If your company pays for any private expenditure of a director or employee this will generally be taxed as a benefit-in-kind and the company will pay Class 1A NI on it at 12.8%. At worst, the Taxman will ask for the additional tax and NI on additional earnings from the company. So when your friend says their company is paying for their own gardening tax-free this is not the full story.

However, how would the Taxman find out that your friend was doing this anyway? For starters, the company has a duty to put such expenditure on an annual benefits declaration. If it doesn't and it's found out, say, during a visit from the Taxman, there will be overdue tax, interest and penalties to pay. Although not totally tax-free, there are still tax savings to be had by having you gardening expenses paid for by your company but treated as a benefit-in-kind.

There is, however, a definite grey area when it comes to indoor gardening.

<u>Office plants</u>

Let's say your company buys some plants from a garden centre to improve the working environment in your office. Is this tax deductible? We think so on the basis that this is an acceptable cost of running a modern day office. The company will also need things like watering cans, watering trays, plant food, sprays, support sticks etc. to help these plants survive the rigours of office life. For those that don't survive, your company will have to buy replacements.

What's to say that some of these potted plants and related items don't end up in your home rather than the office? Or you took them home for emergency recovery treatment and never got around to bringing them back; is this a potential tax problem? The amounts involved are likely to relatively small (a trivial benefit) and so not picked up by either you or the Taxman.

6.2. WHAT IT MIGHT COST

If you go down the route of including gardening maintenance as part of your remuneration package, what will this cost you in tax?

Example

Tony has been too busy to look after his garden. It needs a good blitz to get it into shape. After that it should be easy to maintain. Let's say the blitz will cost him £1,000 - including some tree surgery. But ongoing maintenance is only likely to be £50 per month. He thinks the company's own maintenance contractors do a good job so he asks them if they'll arrange the work for him. Where does he stand for tax if the company pays for the lot?

If classed as a benefit-in-kind, Tony (as a higher-rate taxpayer) might pay income tax of £520 (£1,300 @40%) on the £1,000 blitz plus £300 for six months' ongoing work. The company would also have to pay employers' NI on this benefit of £166 (£1,300 @12.8%). Total tax bill £686 (£520 + £166).

6.3. WHAT ARE THE POTENTIAL TAX SAVINGS?

If you pay for gardening/indoor plants out of your own pocket then it's likely to come from income that has already suffered tax. If it's income from your company this money has probably been extracted as either salary or dividends. If you can reduce your tax bill by getting the company to pay direct then you are in a winning situation. So what are the potential tax savings?

6.3.1. Not treated as additional salary

Example

If, instead of being taxed as a benefit-in-kind, the gardening outlay is classed as additional salary for you, the tax bill goes through the roof. The Taxman will say that to have £1,300 to spend you should have paid tax and NI on a gross addition to your salary from the company. As a 40% taxpayer that's £2,203.39 gross pay (£1,300/59 x 100), so he'll come looking for £903.39 in income tax and employees' NI and £282.03 (£2,203.39 x 12.8%) in employers' NI. Total tax bill £1,185.42. Going down the benefit-in-kind route saves tax of about £500 (£1,185.42 - £686).

Although the company pays employers' NI on the cost to it of the service, this is less than the NI it would pay on the equivalent salary.

6.3.2. Corporation Tax

Your company will get a tax deduction for the expenditure itself and the employers' NI on the benefit-in-kind. You would not get a tax deduction for it. This leaves more money in the company for you to take out at a later stage. **Rule of thumb.** The company will save Corporation Tax on this benefit-in-kind (net of VAT) at the rate of 19%. You will save employees' NI at the rate of either 11% or 1%.

6.4. THE PAPERWORK

You've reassessed your remuneration package to include maintaining your garden as a benefit-in-kind for yourself. What your company therefore needs to do is put this arrangement in writing - both in the company board minutes and as an addition to your contract of employment.

After the end of the tax year, your company then has to get its external reporting right to the Taxman by including this benefit-in-kind on your P11D.

6.4.1. The board minute

Use a board minute to acknowledge this change to your remuneration package.

Example

The board minute covering Jim's "ground force" option reads as follows: "In recognition of your contribution to the company and to avoid you spending time away from company business at key times to undertake gardening duties the company has decided that as part of your remuneration package it will contract and pay for the cost of a maintenance blitz/monthly maintenance for the garden in your principal private residence, up to a value of £1,000 pa. This is, of course, subject to the company having sufficient funds to do so."

You're not trying to hide anything from the Taxman; in fact you want this out in the open and agreed.

Tip. Write to your advisor telling him what you're doing so that it can be included on your P11D. This also helps him in assessing your tax position.

6.4.2. Your contract of employment

Your company needs to put this addition to your remuneration package in writing as an amendment to your contract of employment.

Example

Amendment to contract of employment.

As from November 30, 2006, the company will contract and pay for gardening at your principal private residence up to a specified value to be agreed annually with the company. Anything in excess of this you will reimburse the company for. This benefit-in-kind is from this date part of your remuneration package with the company and will be provided by it subject to the company having sufficient funds to do so.

6.4.3. Contract with/invoice from the supplier

You need the cost of gardening to be treated as a benefit-in-kind. Therefore, the contract with the gardener must be negotiated by, addressed to and clearly seen to be a liability of the company (not yours).

6.4.4. On the VAT return

<u>Making a contribution</u>

Tɪᴘ. If the company has claimed VAT on the gardening costs, pay a nominal sum to it for the ongoing service, say, £10 per month. You don't have to pay this contribution monthly; just one sum before the end of the tax year will do the trick. Treat this as inclusive of VAT and include the output VAT on your company's VAT return. (On £10 that's output VAT of £1.49 (£10 x 17.5/117.5.) Otherwise, the VATman can disallow the company's claim for input VAT on the whole invoice.

Any contribution you make towards the company's cost reduces the potential tax charge both for you and the company.

6.4.5. On your P11D

Your company needs to enter the VAT-inclusive cost(s) (even if it has already claimed the VAT) of maintaining your garden, on your P11D.

6.4.6. In the company's accounts

Transfer the cost of this work out of, say, maintenance and into staff costs. This reinforces your company's argument that it's part of your remuneration package and hence it can claim a tax deduction for this expense.

6.4.7. Your tax return

You simply take the figure given to you by the company for your P11D benefit and put it on your tax return. No further disclosures are required by you.

6.5. LOW, MEDIUM AND HIGH-RISK STRATEGIES

6.5.1. Low-risk

If you get the paperwork right the low-risk strategy is the benefit-in-kind route outlined above.

6.5.2. Medium-risk

The company does not get a tax deduction for the costs of maintaining your garden for you because the Taxman doesn't accept that this expense is "wholly and exclusively" for the purpose of the company's trade. This would be the case if it wasn't clear that this was part of your remuneration package.

6.5.3. High-risk

Your company contracts and pays for "maintenance" work. The invoice is made out for one amount that includes work at all locations (including at your home). Since there is only one invoice to cover the maintenance contract it's going to be difficult for anyone to pick out any private expenditure. You wait six years and hope the Taxman doesn't pick this up before then. If he does, there will be the overdue tax, interest and penalties to pay.

7. Gifts

7.1. THE EXPENSE

Buying gifts for your partner and putting them through the company is obviously a red rag to a bull as far as the Taxman is concerned. He will want his share of tax and NI on what he sees as your remuneration. If he finds out, that is.

The more creative amongst you might do this anyway and then describe the expenses on a petty cash voucher. For example; *"£150 equipment-digital radio for the staff restroom"* or *"£30 flowers for the office"* thus misdirecting any potential challenge to your expenses from your accountant or the Taxman. Whilst we cannot condone this, we, like the Taxman, know it goes on. But why go to all that trouble when there are legitimate ways to get the company to pay for it, particularly if your partner works for the company.

A romantic dinner for two

Any expense for the benefit of staff is normally deductible against the company's profits but taxable on the employee. But there's a concession which could make a meal completely tax-free. Each tax year (April 6 to April 5) the company can spend up to £150 per head on staff events, without any taxable benefit assessed on the employee.

TIP. If your partner is your only employee and you haven't already spent the whole £150 per employee on another event, such as attending a summer concert, then why not have a Christmas party? As long as the total bill for this year's staff events comes to less than £150 per employee, it'll be tax and NI-free for both of you. Try and formalise the outing as a works do by recording the booking in the company minutes. And make sure the company pays directly for the meal otherwise it's an expense to be repaid to you as a director, which may not be allowable.

A diamond ring?

If your partner is also a director or earns at least £8,500 a year from the company (including benefits), then getting the company to buy them, say a diamond ring, as a reward for services could still work out cheaper than paying for it yourself.

Box of chocolates etc.

Although there's technically no monetary limit below which gifts to staff are considered tax-free, the Taxman recognises that some gifts (not money or vouchers) should be ignored as they are so "trivial" in nature that it would cost too much to collect. The examples given in the Taxman's manual include a bottle of wine or a box of chocolates. But the gift must not be seen as a reward for services or it will be taxable.

Tɪᴘ. If your partner works for the company, the gift of a box of chocolates can legitimately be put through the company. Just make sure it's recorded as a goodwill gift.

What's considered a small gift? A turkey or a box of chocolates can cost anything from a couple of pounds to over £30, and a bottle of wine could cost several hundred pounds. Small to one company could be very expensive to another. Do other gifts count? The Taxman has only cited turkeys, chocolates and wine as examples. These would be no use to a teetotal vegetarian on a diet.

Tɪᴘ. Before you (and your employees) receive any trivial benefits, write to your tax office seeking confirmation and agreement that you can leave the benefits you wish to provide off your P11D reporting.

7.2. WHAT ARE THE POTENTIAL TAX SAVINGS?

If you pay for gifts out of your own pocket then it's likely that this comes out of income that's already suffered tax. If it's income from your company this money has probably been extracted as either salary or dividends. If you can reduce your tax bill by getting the company to pay direct then you are in a winning situation. So what are the potential tax savings?

Example 1

To have £300 in your pocket to pay for a nice evening out, it will cost you £75 in income tax (as a higher-rate taxpayer) to take this out of your company as a dividend. Total cost of meal to you: £375. However, if your company pays for a staff event it can claim back any VAT it's been charged and get a tax deduction for all the costs associated with the event. On a £300 bill that's potentially £44.68 (£300 x 17.5/117.5) of recoverable VAT for your company and reduction in its Corporation Tax bill of £48.51 (£300 - £44.68 = £255.32 at 19%). Net cost of the event to the company £206.81. Total saving £168.19.

Example 2

If you pay for a diamond ring for your partner out of dividends, then, as a higher-rate taxpayer, you'll have to pay tax on those dividends at 25%. So, if you take £1,000 out as dividends, your tax bill will be £250. However, if the company pays directly for the ring, it can be included on your partner's P11D, they (well, you on their behalf) will pay 22% tax on the benefit (£220) and the company will pay 12.8% NI (£128). However, as long as you can prove the gift is for business purposes (record it in the company minutes as a reward for services), the company will get 19% tax relief for the gift plus NI (19% of £1,128 = £214) so the overall tax paid is £134. A saving of £116.

7.3. THE PAPERWORK

Your company has to get its internal and external reporting right.

7.3.1. The board minute

In a board minute include a commercial reason for the company agreeing to include specific gifts as part of the remuneration package.

Example

The board minute reads as follows: "In recognition of your contribution, the company has decided that as part of your remuneration package, it will contract and pay for an item of personal jewellery, up to a value of £1,000. This is, of course, subject to the company having sufficient funds to do so."

You're not trying to hide anything from the Taxman; in fact you want this out in the open and agreed.

Tip. Write to your advisor telling him what you're doing so that it can be included on your P11D.

7.3.2. Your contract of employment

Your company needs to put any addition to your remuneration package in writing as an amendment to your contract of employment.

Example

Amendment to contract of employment
As from November 30, 2006, the company will contract and pay for an item of personal jewellery, up to a value of £1,000. This is, of course, subject to the company having sufficient funds to do so.

7.3.3. Contract with/invoice from the supplier

You need the jewellery to be treated as a benefit-in-kind. As such the contract with the jeweller needs to be negotiated by, addressed to, and be clearly a liability of the company (not yours).

7.3.4. On the VAT return

Staff events

If a guest comes to an event ask them to pay a nominal contribution towards costs, say, £10. Treat this as inclusive of VAT and include the output VAT on your company's VAT return. (On £10 that's output VAT of £1.49 (£10 x 17.5/117.5.) Otherwise, the VATman can disallow the company's claim for input VAT on the guest's share of the costs.

You can also legitimately give staff gifts, up to the value of £50 plus VAT in any twelve-month period, and claim back any VAT you were charged in buying them.

7.3.5. On your P11D

Your company needs to enter the VAT-inclusive cost(s) (even if the company has already claimed the VAT) of the gift on your P11D.

7.3.6. In the company's accounts

Transfer the cost of this gift out of general expenses (if that's where it's ended up) and into staff costs. This reinforces your company's argument that it is part of your remuneration package and hence it can claim a tax deduction for it.

7.3.7. Your tax return

You simply take whatever the figure given to you by the company for your P11D benefits and put them on your tax return. No further disclosures are required by you.

7.4. LOW, MEDIUM AND HIGH-RISK STRATEGIES

7.4.1. Low-risk

Putting gifts for yourself through your company's expenses is risky.

However, treating your spouse (as a member of staff) to a meal can legitimately be claimed if it's part of a staff event.

A potential tax liability exists with even minor gifts. However, it seems the Taxman will not bother to collect it. Write to your tax office asking permission to leave specific trivial benefits off your company's P11Ds.

7.4.2. Medium-risk

The company doesn't get a tax deduction for the costs of gifts to staff because the Taxman doesn't accept that this expense is "wholly and exclusively" for the purpose of the company's trade. This would be the case if it wasn't clear that this was a staff event or a goodwill gesture to staff or that it's part of your remuneration package.

7.4.3. High-risk

Describe the presents on a petty cash voucher. For example, *"£150 equipment-digital radio for the staff restroom"* (actually at home) or *"£30 flowers for the office"* (they were for your partner) thus misdirecting any potential challenge to your expenses from your accountant or the Taxman. You then wait six years and hope the Taxman doesn't pick this up before then. If he does, there will be the overdue tax, interest and penalties to pay.

8. Language lessons

8.1. THE EXPENSE

Your company can get a full tax deduction for any work-related training it provides to its employees, which includes you as a director. "Work-related" means any skill you may have need of at work either now or in the future (or even when you work in a voluntary capacity on behalf of the firm, such as helping a local charity).

For example, as almost any company with a website can expect to receive product enquiries from other countries, so foreign language skills are necessary for all staff, particularly those who may need to negotiate overseas contracts.

The range of courses the company can pay for is quite extensive. For example, if your staff have to drive as part of their job you can provide advanced driving lessons, or for trainees who don't yet hold a driving licence you can pay for a full driving course including the test fees.

8.2. WHAT IT MIGHT COST

You can expect to pay about £50 per week for two hours' instruction from a qualified teacher, for at least ten weeks, to achieve fluency. Interestingly, there won't be any tax cost associated with this being paid for by your company if it's work-related.

8.3. WHAT ARE THE POTENTIAL TAX SAVINGS?

Example

Let's say you pay about £50 per week for two hours' instruction from a qualified teacher, for at least ten weeks. That's £500 from your after-tax income, which to put you in funds to do so will cost your company £911 in gross wages and NI (£500/59% = £847 gross wages + £64 employers' NI), or £738 after Corporation Tax (CT) relief at 19%.

If your company contracts directly with your language teacher to provide your personal lessons, the cost to it will be £500, but that expense will be fully tax deductible as staff training. So the net cost to a company paying 19% CT is £405 (81% x £500). That's a 45% saving for your company ((£738 - £405)/£738) compared with paying you extra salary.

8.4. THE PAPERWORK

Trap. If the employee picks up the cost of the course and you reimburse those fees, the amount paid will be taxed as a benefit-in-kind.

Tip. The contract for the training course must always be between the provider of the course (driving school, University etc.) and the employing company, not between the course provider and the employee.

What your company needs to do is put this internal arrangement in writing - both in the company board minutes and as a company policy document.

8.4.1. The board minute

In your board minute include a commercial reason for the company agreeing to courses for employees (including directors).

Example

The board minute agreeing to "work-related" training might reads as follows:

"The company has decided to provide work-related training for its employees, which includes directors. "Work-related" means any skill the employee may have need of at work either now or in the future, or even when the employee works in a voluntary capacity on behalf of the firm. In particular, via our website we expect to receive product enquiries from other countries, so foreign language skills are necessary for all staff, particularly those, such as the directors, who may need to negotiate overseas contracts. This is, of course, subject to the company having sufficient funds to do so."

You're not trying to hide anything from the Taxman; in fact you want this out in the open and agreed.

Tip. Write to your advisor telling him what you're doing so that it can be excluded from your P11D, under the exemption for work-related training.

8.4.2. Your contract of employment

Your company needs to put the availability of work-related training in writing as an amendment to your contract of employment.

> *Example*
>
> *Amendment to contract of employment*
> *As from November 30, 2006, the company will, from time to time, contract and pay for work-related training. This will be provided by it subject to the company having sufficient funds to do so.*

8.4.3. Contract with/invoice from the supplier

You need the work-related training course to be a contractual liability of the company, not your own. As such, the contract with the course provider needs to be negotiated by, addressed to and clearly be seen as a liability of the company (not yours).

8.4.4. On the VAT return

Any VAT charged by the course provider can be claimed back by your company on its VAT return.

8.4.5. On your P11D

No entry required.

8.4.6. In the company's accounts

Book the course costs under something like "training" or "staff costs".

8.4.7. Your tax return

No entry required

8.5. LOW, MEDIUM AND HIGH-RISK STRATEGIES

8.5.1. Low-risk

If you get the paperwork right the low-risk strategy is the one outlined above.

8.5.2. Medium-risk

The company doesn't get a tax deduction for the costs of such training because the Taxman doesn't accept that this expense does not meet the conditions of the exemption. This would be the case if the course wasn't for a skill needed at work.

8.5.3. High-risk

You book a course of flying or scuba diving lessons in your own name, but have the company pay for them. Booked as staff training in your accounts no entries are made on your P11D in the relevant tax year. You now wait six years and hope the Taxman doesn't pick this up before then. If he does, there will be the overdue tax, interest and penalties to pay.

9. Magazine subscriptions

9.1. THE EXPENSE

The Taxman publishes a list of those subscriptions which he considers you can get a tax deduction for. This can be found at http://www.inlandrevenue.gov.uk/subs. But what this doesn't tell you is whether the subscription to your favourite magazine is tax deductible.

Subscriptions to magazines, newspapers etc. will be deductible if they are "wholly and exclusively" for the purpose of the trade. Classic examples of this are subscriptions to business-to-business publications like monthly trade magazines. But what about your newspapers/favourite magazines (Top Gear, Hello etc.) you get at home? Not really tax deductible unless…

You probably have a reception area in the office for visitors, or a staff restroom where it would be logical to have a pile of magazines to read and keep up-to-date.

TIP. Get the company to pay direct for your favourite magazines or reimburse you for them. These can either be delivered to the office or you bring them in from home. Either way they end up in reception or the restroom. That's what the company bought them for wasn't it?

And another thing. With that many magazines what are you going to keep them in? How about a nice antique oak magazine/newspaper rack? Paid for by the company of course but very similar to the one you've got at home. Your company, your taste.

9.2. WHAT IT MIGHT COST

How much is an annual subscription? Your company could probably get a "12 issues for the price of 10, plus a free gift" offer, as a new subscriber to a publication. So if each magazine had an issue price of £3.50, the cost to your company would be £35 for an annual subscription.

9.3. WHAT ARE THE POTENTIAL TAX SAVINGS?

If you pay for the magazine subscription out of your own pocket then it's likely to be from income that's already suffered tax. If it's income from your company this money has probably been extracted as either salary or dividends. If you can reduce your tax bill by getting the company to pay direct then you are in a winning situation. So what are the potential tax savings?

> *Example*
>
> *Some car magazines can cost £4.00 a month, that's £48 a year. Four of these gets you to nearly £200 a year. If you pay out, say, as a 40% taxpayer, that's gross salary of about £333 (£200x100/60). If the company pays for it but puts it down as a benefit-in-kind, you could end up paying tax of £80 (£200x40%). So let the company pay for it and include it under staff welfare costs - along with the tea, coffee etc. It's just another office expense. There's no tax bill for you this way.*

9.4. THE PAPERWORK

9.4.1. Contract with/invoice from the supplier

You need the publication to be treated as "wholly and exclusively" for the business. As such, the subscription with the publisher/newsagent needs to be addressed to and clearly be a liability of the company (not yours).

9.4.2. On your P11D

No entry required.

9.4.3. In the company's accounts

Include magazines under, say, staff welfare costs - along with the tea, coffee etc. It's just another office expense.

9.4.4. Your tax return

No entry required.

9.5. LOW, MEDIUM AND HIGH-RISK STRATEGIES

9.5.1. Low-risk

Your company buys magazines for the office, which you read second-hand.

9.5.2. Medium-risk

The company does not get a tax deduction for the costs of magazine subscriptions because the Taxman doesn't accept that this expense is "wholly and exclusively" for the purpose of the company's trade. This would be the case if it wasn't clear that this was part of a normal business activity.

9.5.3. High-risk

If your favourite magazine ends up at the office, who's to say it's not part of general office costs. So get the company to pay for the subscription to the magazine, you just act as postman.

10. Paying for a holiday

10.1. THE EXPENSE

You need a holiday. Having decided you are definitely going you might well ask yourself the question, why is it that my company can't just pay for this well-earned break?

It's perfectly legal for the company to pay for a director's or employee's holiday and get a tax deduction for it against the company's profits for Corporation Tax (CT) purposes, as long as the payment gets taxed as part of their remuneration package

10.2. WHAT IT MIGHT COST

Example

Let's take a £2,000 holiday to be either funded out of net salary, paid direct by your company or covered by a special dividend.

	Salary (£)	Benefit (£)	Dividend (£)
Holiday cost	2,000	2,000	2,000
Income tax and EEs' NI	1,390	800	500
ERs' NI	434	256	-
Total cost	3,824	3,056	2,500
CT saving (*)	(727)	(429)	-
Net cost	**3,097**	**2,627**	**2,500**

(*) CT saving on : Salary of £726.56 = £3,824x19%
Benefit-in-kind of £428.64 = £2,256x19%.

If the company paid you an additional salary to cover the cost of a holiday it would get a CT deduction for this salary (plus employers' NI cost). But this can work out a bit expensive. A £2,000 holiday would require a gross salary before taxes of say £3,390 (£2,000x100/59) and result in an employers' NI bill of £433.92 (£3,390x12.8%). The company spends £3,823.92.

10.3. WHAT ARE THE POTENTIAL TAX SAVINGS?

If you pay for the holiday out of your own pocket then it's likely that this comes out of income that has already suffered tax. If it's income from your company this money has probably been extracted as either salary or dividends. If you can reduce your tax bill by getting the company to pay direct then you are in a winning situation. So what are the potential tax savings?

Example

A trip invoiced to and paid for in the company's name is potentially a benefit-in-kind, i.e. it's not capable of conversion into cash by you. A £2,000 holiday would cost you £800 (£2,000x40%) in additional income tax and your company NI on the benefit-in-kind, i.e. 12.8% of £2,000=£256. The company spends £2,256 and the Taxman collects £800 from you. The CT saving is £428.64 (£2,256x19%).

A dividend of £2,000 would save on NI compared to a benefit-in-kind but is not tax deductible.

10.4. THE PAPERWORK

You've reassessed your remuneration package to include in it a holiday expense you would like the company to incur as a benefit-in-kind for yourself. What your company needs to do is put this arrangement in writing - both amongst the company board minutes and as an addition to your contract of employment.

Once the holiday has been completed, your company then has to get its external reporting right, first to the VATman, then in its accounts and finally to the Taxman on its P11D.

10.4.1. The board minute

In your board minute include a commercial reason for the company agreeing to include holiday arrangements as part of your remuneration package.

Example

The board minute covering Jim's holiday reads as follows: "In recognition of your contribution to the company and the need to take a break to renew your enthusiasm and freshness for your day-to-day tasks, the company has decided that as part of your remuneration package, it will contract and pay for one two-week holiday each year.

> *However, this must be taken during the company's deemed quiet period which is currently the month of August. This is, of course, subject to the company having sufficient funds to do so."*

You're not trying to hide anything from the Taxman; in fact you want this out in the open and agreed.

TIP. Write to your advisor telling him what you're doing so that it can be included on your P11D.

10.4.2. Your contract of employment

Your company needs to put this addition to your remuneration package in writing as an amendment to your contract of employment.

> *Example*
>
> *Amendment to contract of employment*
> *As from November 30, 2006, the company will contract and pay for a two-week holiday each year. However, this must be taken during the company's deemed quiet period, which is currently the month of August. This benefit-in-kind is from that date part of your remuneration package with the company and will be provided by it subject to the company having sufficient funds to do so.*

10.4.3. Contract with/invoice from the supplier

You need the holiday to be treated as a benefit-in-kind. As such the contract with the travel agent needs to be negotiated by, addressed to and clearly be seen as the liability of the company.

10.4.4. On the VAT return

Don't bother to claim the VAT back on the holiday.

10.4.5. On your P11D

Your company needs to enter the cost of the holiday in that tax year on your P11D.

10.4.6. In the company's accounts

Transfer the cost of this holiday out of travel and subsistence expenses and into staff costs. This reinforces your company's argument that it's part of your remuneration package and hence it can claim a tax deduction for it.

10.4.7. Your tax return

You simply take the figure given to you by the company for your P11D benefit and put it on your tax return. No further disclosures are required by you.

10.5. LOW, MEDIUM AND HIGH-RISK STRATEGIES

10.5.1. Low-risk

If you get the paperwork right the low-risk strategy is the one outlined above.

10.5.2. Medium-risk

The company does not get a tax deduction for the costs of the holiday because the Taxman doesn't accept that this expense is "wholly and exclusively" for the purpose of the company's trade. This would be the case if it wasn't clear that this was part of your remuneration package.

10.5.3. High-risk

It's easy enough to identify the payment for a package holiday e.g. an entry on the company credit card statement for £2,000 for Happy Holidays Limited. However, if you book it yourself with separate payments for flights, car hire and hotel accommodation you end up with different invoices/payments at different times to different companies. That's not so easy to trace.

When, say, the company credit card statement is analysed these company expenses could end up in travel (flights), motor expenses (car hire) and accommodation (hotel). All could be forgotten by the time it comes to preparing the company accounts, say, twelve months later. If these individual amounts don't stick out from the crowd within those expense headings, who's going to spot them?

It's an option but a risky one of course because of interest and penalties for not accounting to the Taxman for tax on either the additional salary to cover the holiday payments or the benefit-in-kind.

You could transfer the costs to your director's loan account to avoid penalties etc., but this would only be a temporary solution.

11. Private tutors

11.1. THE EXPENSE

Saturday morning ballet or karate lessons were probably not what the government had in mind when it gave tax relief for childcare paid for by employers. But the Taxman has confirmed that as long as the teacher is an approved childcarer, any different activities (such as personal tuition) offered in the course of providing the childcare, will still be covered by the tax exemption. So how is this possible?

All employers can give their employees childcare vouchers, or pay for childcare directly worth up to £55 per week, with no tax or NI charges. This tax-free limit is per employee not per child, so if you have more than one child, or your spouse doesn't work, you lose out. This can be used for your child's education as well as care, as long as certain conditions are met.

Condition 1. The childcare vouchers, or direct payment by the company must be used for qualifying care provided before September 1 following the child's 15th birthday. This is generally the beginning of the school year 11/end of year 10/the final year of compulsory schooling. So you can't use this tax break to pay for last minute GCSE or A-level exam tuition.

Qualifying care can be any form of care or supervised activity that is not part of the child's compulsory education. So as long as the subject of your child's extra lessons is not covered in compulsory school hours, it can be paid for directly by your company or with childcare vouchers up to the tax-free limit.

Condition 2. The care must be provided by a registered or approved childcarer. Unfortunately, most registered childminders are not also qualified to teach music, karate, Latin or whatever extra skill you want your child to learn.

However, specialist private teachers can register with the Department for Education and Skills to become an approved childcarer if they provide their services in England (different regulations apply in Scotland and Wales). To do this the teacher must have; **(1)** a basic childcare qualification; **(2)** hold a first aid certificate appropriate to children and;

(3) have a clean enhanced criminal records check. All of which you'd probably look for in a private tutor anyway.

If your company reimburses you for the tutor's fees, or pays a bill made out to you personally, the tax exemption doesn't apply.

Tɪᴘ. Once a specialist private teacher has registered with the Department for Education and Skills to become an approved childcarer, get your company to make arrangements directly with them for the lessons to be provided to your child, and sign any contract required. The full cost of the lessons is then tax deductible for the company and the first £55 per week is tax and NI-free for you.

11.2. WHAT IT MIGHT COST

Because of the exemption for childcare vouchers there is no tax cost to you. Indeed, if you and your partner both work for the company that's a tax-free limit of £110 per week.

11.3. WHAT ARE THE POTENTIAL TAX SAVINGS?

If you pay for the tuition out of your own pocket then it's likely that this comes out of income that has already suffered tax. If it's income from your company this money has probably been extracted as either salary or dividends. If you can reduce your tax bill by getting the company to pay direct then you are in a winning situation.

11.4. THE PAPERWORK

You've reassessed your remuneration package to include childcare vouchers, as a benefit-in-kind for yourself. What your company needs to do is put this arrangement in writing - as a new company policy, amongst the company board minutes and as an addition to your contract of employment.

11.5. THE CHILDCARE POLICY

Your company will need to have a written policy on childcare vouchers.

Example

The Company operates a childcare voucher scheme which is open to all employees. The scheme is implemented as a salary sacrifice arrangement where you exchange part of your salary for childcare vouchers.

The first £55 per week of the voucher's face value will be given to you tax and NI-free as long as the following conditions are met...... (same conditions as for the Taxman).

You will provide details of your childcare provider to the Company including their registration or approval number together with the date the relevant registration expires.

You must notify the Company of any changes in registration or approval status of your child's carer or changes in childcare arrangements.

The Company will provide you with a childcare voucher. You will then give this voucher to your qualifying childcare provider. The childcare provider will then sign the voucher and send it to the Company for reimbursement. There is no cost to the childcare provider in receiving payment through childcare vouchers.

11.5.1. Your contract of employment

Your company needs to put this addition to your remuneration package in writing as an amendment to your contract of employment.

Example

Amendment to contract of employment
As from November 30, 2006, you are entitled to opt for childcare vouchers as part of your remuneration package. This benefit-in-kind will be provided by the company subject to it having sufficient funds to do so.

11.5.2. On your P11D

No entry required within the £55 per week limit.

11.5.3. In the company's accounts

Record the cost of these childcare vouchers as "staff costs".

11.5.4. Your tax return

No entry required within the £55 per week limit.

11.6. LOW, MEDIUM AND HIGH-RISK STRATEGIES

11.6.1. Low-risk

If you get the paperwork right the low-risk strategy is the one outlined above.

11.6.2. Medium-risk

The company does not get a tax deduction for the childcare vouchers because the Taxman doesn't accept that this expense is "wholly and exclusively" for the purpose of the company's trade. This would be the case if it wasn't clear that this was part of your remuneration package.

11.6.3. High-risk

Your company settles your account with a private tutor but records this as staff training. No entries are made on your P11D or tax return. You now wait six years and hope the Taxman doesn't pick this up before then. If he does, there will be the overdue tax, interest and penalties to pay.

12. School fees

12.1. THE EXPENSE

With the cost of a private education running into thousands of pounds per term it would be nice if you could get the company to foot the bill. But if a company meets the personal liability of a director or other employee then the Taxman will apply the "pecuniary liability principle" and there will be penalties added for not making the right declarations. But by following the rules set out below you can get your children's education paid for by the company without paying tax at penal rates.

12.2. WHAT ARE THE POTENTIAL TAX SAVINGS?

If you pay the tuition fees yourself it will come from income that's already had tax deducted from it. However, if the company pays then you save some of the tax. The potential savings are examined below.

12.2.1. Savings on your salary

If the company pays for your child's education, the payments will be taxed under the benefit-in-kind rules on you as the director/employee.

The tax on this benefit will be less than what you would have normally paid under PAYE to get the same net amount of income to meet the school fees yourself. In addition, there won't be any employees' NI to pay either. The company will have an NI bill to pay, but once again it will be on a lesser amount than the salary equivalent.

12.2.2. Corporation tax

Your company will be permitted to make a deduction in its accounts for the school fees, which means it pays less Corporation Tax. And because it's classed as a remuneration, the NI paid by the company on the benefit-in-kind gets tax relief too, leaving more money in the company for you to take out at a later date.

12.3. EXAMPLE

If the annual school fees were £15,000, this is the level of additional salary you would require after tax and NI has been deducted by the company. We can now compare the relative tax positions if the £15,000 is treated as net salary or as a benefit-in-kind.

12.3.1. You

	22% TAXPAYER	40% TAXPAYER
Tax on salary £15,000 (x 33/67) or (x 41/59)	7,388	10,423
Tax on benefits of £15,000	3,300	6,000
Saving	**4,088**	**4,423**

12.3.2. Your company and NI

	22% TAXPAYER	40% TAXPAYER
NI on salary @ 12.8%	2,865	3,254
NI on benefits @ 12.8%	1,920	1,920
Saving	**946**	**1,344**

12.3.3. Corporation Tax saving on a benefit

	40% TAXPAYER
Corporation Tax on annual school fees (£15,000 @ 19%)	2,850
Corporation Tax on NI (£1,920 @ 19%)	365
Saving	**3,215**

12.4. THE PAPERWORK

By taking the following steps you will make sure that there is no room for a challenge by the Taxman. And with all the paperwork in order there should be no risk of penalties arising at a later date either.

12.4.1. The board minute

Remember, any expense charged in the company's accounts has to meet the "wholly and exclusively" test. Getting a formal board minute drawn up demonstrates to the Taxman that the benefit was agreed on by the company as a way of rewarding you for your services to the company. There is no need for any special wording, just a statement of the facts as a record for future reference.

Example

The following can be used as an example:

"Meeting of the Board of Directors of XYZ Limited on .... at ....

It was resolved that the company approve the payment of school fees of Mr X's children as part of his remuneration package.

This award has been made in recognition of his continuing contribution to the success of the company.

Signed .... company secretary."

12.4.2. Your contract of employment

Because this is a variation of your remuneration package you will need to incorporate it into your contract of employment by way of an addendum.

Example

"As of .... the company will pay your children's school fees subject to the availability of funds. This benefit-in-kind is to be treated as part of your remuneration package with the company."

12.4.3. Contract with/invoice from the supplier

You need to get the school to make it absolutely clear that the liability for payment rests with the company and that they will not revert to you should there be any delay in settling the fees.

12.4.4. On the VAT return

Because there's no VAT chargeable on the provision of education there will be no VAT to reclaim on the school fees.

12.4.5. On your P11D

The value of the benefit-in-kind to be included in your P11D is the contracted value of the school fees in that tax year.

12.4.6. In the company's accounts

Although there are no special disclosure requirements, if you include the charge for the school fees within remuneration costs, this reinforces your position that it's part of your agreed package.

12.4.7. Your tax return

Simply transfer the values from your P11D to the relevant boxes on your tax return's employment pages. Any tax due will then be collected in the normal way.

12.5. LOW, MEDIUM AND HIGH-RISK STRATEGIES

12.5.1. Low-risk

If you get the paperwork right, the low-risk strategy is the one outlined above.

12.5.2. Medium-risk

The company does not get a tax deduction for the costs of school fees because the Taxman doesn't accept that this expense is "wholly and exclusively" for the purpose of the company's trade. This would be the case if it wasn't clear that this was part of your remuneration package.

The Taxman might be happy to include the payment of school fees as part of your remuneration package, but as earnings instead of as a benefit-in-kind. How is this possible? If the ultimate liability for school fees is with the parents (as insisted upon by the school) then the company is settling your pecuniary liability. This is earnings not a benefit-in-kind. Big tax bill!

If there is any doubt, you're better off taking an extra dividend instead to meet the school fees (provided the company has enough post-tax (at 19%) profits to do so).

12.5.3. High-risk

A high-risk strategy here would be to pay the school fees without declaring anything to the Taxman. You will get away with paying no tax on the benefits and having the tax relief on the fees.

However, if discovered, the Taxman will hit the company with a bill for the tax and NI on the net benefits grossed up to the "salary" value. In addition, there will be the company NI bill, plus fines for incorrect P11Ds and interest for late payment. This is because it will be deemed that the company has met a personal liability of an employee.

13. Personal trainer

13.1. THE EXPENSE

Joining a gym isn't cheap - it can cost anywhere between £600 and £1,000 a year. And paying £1,000 out of taxed income is the equivalent of receiving a bonus from your company of £1,695 (£1,000/59%). So is it cheaper if the company pays for it instead?

The normal rules are that if the company pays for your subscription, e.g. to a fitness club, then you will still be taxed on the value of the subscription and the company will have to pay National Insurance (NI) at 12.8%. However, even though you may be taxed on the subscription, it could still be worth your while getting the company to pay for it. And unlike salary, you have no NI to pay.

Just the NI savings make it cheaper for your company to pay the gym membership on your behalf. But there are even greater savings to be had if it can be treated as a tax-free benefit. In simple terms, sports and recreational "facilities" can be provided tax-free if they are; **(1)** generally available to all employees; **(2)** not on domestic premises; and **(3)** not a facility available to the public generally.

Tɪᴘ **1.** Rather than join a gym, why not hire a personal fitness trainer as the "sports facility"? At, say, £30 a session two days a week, that's about £240 a month tax-free. Just make sure the option of hiring the trainer is open to all employees (perhaps as part of their benefits package).

Tɪᴘ **2.** If you belong to a business group why not club together with the other members and hire a local gym or health club for exclusive use for your employees on, say, certain evenings, so excluding the members of the public at those times?

Tɪᴘ **3.** If the expense is part of your remuneration package with your company then it's generally tax deductible for it as part of staff costs. So why not have a personal trainer as part of that package? This is cheaper for you and is deductible for your company.

13.2. WHAT ARE THE POTENTIAL TAX SAVINGS?

If you pay for a personal fitness trainer out of your own money then it's likely to be income that's already suffered tax. If it's income from your company this money has probably been extracted as either salary or dividends. If you can reduce your tax bill by getting the company to pay direct then you are in a winning situation. So what could be the potential tax savings?

> *Example*
>
> *Fitter Limited pays £600 a year for a health club subscription for one of its directors. As the director is a higher-rate taxpayer, he would have to receive extra salary of £1,017 (£600/59%) to provide the equivalent benefit and the company would have to pay £130 (£1,017 x 12.8%) NI on this extra salary. However, by the company paying the £600 subscription, it pays NI of only £77 (£600 x 12.8%) and the director pays tax of £240. And, unlike salary, the director has no NI to pay.*

TIP. To get the NI savings, make sure the company contracts directly with the personal trainer. If you pay first and then the company reimburses you, this will be treated as additional salary and any potential tax savings will be lost.

13.2.1. Corporation Tax

Your company will get a tax deduction for the expenditure itself and the employers' NI on your benefit-in-kind. You would not get a tax deduction. This leaves more money in the company for you to take out at a later stage. **Rule of thumb.** The company will save Corporation Tax on this benefit-in-kind (net of VAT) at the rate of 19%. You will save employees' NI at the rate of either 11% or 1%.

13.3. THE PAPERWORK

You've reassessed your remuneration package to include a personal fitness trainer as a benefit-in-kind for yourself. What your company needs to do is put this arrangement in writing - both amongst the company board minutes and as an addition to your contract of employment.

Your company will have to get its external reporting right both in its accounts and to the Taxman as part of its annual expenses and benefits reporting (P11Ds etc.).

13.3.1. The board minute

In your board minute you could even add a commercial reason for the company agreeing to include the personal trainer arrangement as part of your remuneration package.

Example

The company is concerned at the lack of energy being displayed by its employees. As from November 30, 2006, the company will contract and pay for a personal trainer to be available to all staff, subject to a maximum consultation of five hours a week for each employee. Consultations to take place outside of office hours in the employee's own time. This benefit-in-kind is from that date part of their remuneration package with the company and will be provided subject to the company having sufficient funds to do so. The impact of this fit-for-work campaign will be reviewed at the end of twelve months.

You're not trying to hide anything from the Taxman; in fact you want this out in the open and agreed.

TIP. Write to your advisor telling him what you're thinking of doing so that it can eventually be included on your P11D.

13.3.2. Your contract of employment

If you can't get a tax exemption making the personal trainer available to all staff (including you), then your company needs to include this benefit as an addition to your remuneration package.

Example

Amendment to contract of employment
As from November 30, 2006, the company will contract and pay for a personal trainer to be available to you, subject to a maximum consultation of five hours a week out of normal office hours. This benefit-in-kind is from that date and this part of your remuneration package with the company will be provided by it subject to the company having sufficient funds to do so.

13.3.3. Contract with/invoice from the supplier

You need the personal trainer's services to be treated as a benefit-in-kind. Any contract with a fitness guru needs to be negotiated by, addressed to and clearly seen to be a liability of the company.

13.3.4. On the VAT return

As long as the "personal trainer" facility is made available to all employees, the company can recover the VAT.

13.3.5. On your P11D

Your company needs to enter the VAT-inclusive cost(s) (even if the company has already claimed the VAT) of the personal trainer on your own P11D. This is if you haven't been able to use the "available to all employees" get out clause.

13.3.6. In the company's accounts

Book the cost of this "fit for work" initiative to "staff costs". This reinforces your company's argument that it is part of a remuneration package and hence it can claim a tax deduction for it.

13.3.7. Your tax return

You simply take the figure given to you by the company for your P11D benefit and put it on your tax return. No further disclosures are required by you.

13.4. LOW, MEDIUM AND HIGH-RISK STRATEGIES

13.4.1. Low-risk

The company can pay but make sure that the personal trainer facility is open to all employees.

13.4.2. Medium-risk

The company does not get a tax deduction for the costs of a personal trainer because the Taxman doesn't accept that this expense is "wholly and exclusively" for the purpose of the company's trade. This would be the case if it wasn't clear that this was part of your company's policy towards all staff.

13.4.3. High-risk

You keep the personal trainer all to yourself but claim the tax exemption (and hence no P11D reporting) as if it were available to all staff. You now wait six years and hope the Taxman doesn't pick this up before then. If he does, there will be the overdue tax, interest and penalties to pay.

14. Cars for the family

14.1. THE EXPENSE

Let's say that one of your dependants needs a car but they cannot afford the cost of running it. They don't work for your company and so wouldn't be entitled to a company car in their own right. You would like to help but if you give them the money it will be after you have paid tax and NI at, say, 41%, which makes it an expensive option for you.

In these circumstances it might be tax-effective for you to have two company cars but let them use one. If a second company-owned car is made available for private use as part of your remuneration package the company can pay for all the repairs, running costs and even the insurance and claim Corporation Tax relief on these expenses as well as the car itself. The catch is a benefit-in-kind charge on you for a second car. So how much tax will this cost you?

14.2. WHAT IT MIGHT COST

The taxable benefit of company cars is based on their CO_2 emissions ratings. The lower the rating, the lower the percentage of list price used to calculate the taxable benefit of having a company car. It starts at 15% for cars with 140g/km and increases by 1% for each 5g/km thereafter up to a 35% maximum.

> ### Example
>
> *If your company buys, say, a Vauxhall Corsa Life 1.0i 12v three door list price £8,835 (which has a CO_2 emissions of 127g/km) and makes this available for private use by your son or daughter, the tax cost to you as a benefit-in-kind would be £8,835 x 15% = £1,325.25 taxable on you at 40% = £530.10. That's the cost of the car plus all its running costs for just over £500! The savings can be greater for more expensive cars.*

TIP. If the second car arrives as a present in, say, October, the tax cost for 2006/7 will be even less because the car will have only been available for just six months of the tax year.

The company will also have to pay employers' NI at 12.8% on the value of this car benefit.

14.3. WHAT ARE THE POTENTIAL TAX SAVINGS?

Obviously, your company has to pay for the financing and running costs of the car. However, this is going to work out cheaper from a tax point of view than drawing the money out of your company, paying tax on that and using the net of tax amount to fund the car personally.

TIP. Your company would also get a 100% tax deduction for the cost of the car if it has an emissions rating of 120g/km or less. Otherwise it would be 25% up to a maximum of £3,000 for cars costing over £12,000.

14.4. THE PAPERWORK

To avoid any quibble with the Taxman, have this second car recorded as part of your remuneration package with the company. It's tax deductible for the company "wholly and exclusively" to keep its key member of staff (you) happy.

You've reassessed your remuneration package to include in it a second company car as a benefit-in-kind for yourself. What your company needs to do is put this arrangement in writing - both amongst the company board minutes and as an addition to your contract of employment.

Once the car has been acquired, your company then has to get its external reporting right, first by notifying the Taxman of a new company car and secondly by calculating the benefit-in-kind on its P11D.

14.4.1. The board minute

In your board minute include a commercial reason for the company agreeing to add a second company car to your remuneration package.

Example

The board minute covering Jim's second car reads as follows: "In recognition of your contribution to the company and to avoid sharing your company car with other members of your family, the company has decided that as part of your remuneration package, it will make available for your private use a second company car. This is, of course, subject to the company being able to finance both the acquisition cost and running expenses of this second vehicle.

You're not trying to hide anything from the Taxman; in fact you want this out in the open and agreed.

Tip. Write to your advisor telling him what you're doing so that it can be included on your P11D.

14.4.2. Your contract of employment

Your company needs to put this addition to your remuneration package in writing as an amendment to your contract of employment.

> *Example*
>
> *Amendment to contract of employment*
> *As from November 30, 2006, the company will make available to you a second company car. This benefit-in-kind is from that date part of your remuneration package with the company and will be provided by it subject to the company being able to finance both the acquisition cost and running expenses.*

14.4.3. Notifying the Taxman of an additional car

To add credibility to the company's planned intention to provide you with a second company car, send in a completed P46 (Car) Form to the Taxman.

14.4.4. On your P11D

Your company needs to disclose the taxable benefit figure for both cars on your P11D, which has to be submitted to the Taxman by July 6 each year.

14.4.5. Your tax return

You simply take the figure given to you by the company for your P11D benefit (for both company cars) and put this on your tax return. No further disclosures are required by you.

14.5. LOW, MEDIUM AND HIGH-RISK STRATEGIES

14.5.1. Low-risk

If you get the paperwork right the low-risk strategy is the one outlined above.

14.5.2. Medium-risk

The company won't get a tax deduction for the cost of your second company car because the Taxman doesn't accept that this expense is "wholly and exclusively" for the purpose of the company's trade. This would be the case if it wasn't clear that this was part of your remuneration package.

14.5.3. High-risk

You put the second company car down as a pool car - but it isn't! You wait six years and hope the Taxman doesn't pick this up before then. If he does, there will be the overdue tax, interest and penalties to pay.

15. Wine

15.1. THE EXPENSE

Buying fine wine on a regular basis is something that many more people are doing these days. You've heard from a colleague that they get their company to foot the bill. How can this be possible, when you consider the rule that if a company meets the personal liability of a director or other employee then the Taxman will treat such a payment as earnings? The relevant tax and NI would be charged on the "grossing up" principles, and there would be penalties added for not having made the right declarations in the first place. However, by following the rules set out below you can get your cases of wine paid for by the company without paying tax at penal rates.

15.2. WHAT ARE THE POTENTIAL TAX SAVINGS?

If you pay for the wine yourself it will come from income that's already had tax deducted from it. However, if the company pays then you save some of the tax that you would have paid on that income withdrawal. The potential savings are examined below.

15.2.1. Saving on salary

If the company pays for your wine, the payments it makes will be taxed under the benefit-in-kind rules on you as the director/employee of the company.

The tax on this benefit will be less than you would have normally paid under PAYE to get the same net amount of income to make the purchase yourself.

In addition there won't be any employees' NI to pay either. The company will have an NI bill to pay, but once again it will be on a lesser amount than the salary equivalent.

15.2.2. Corporation tax

Your company will be permitted to make a deduction in its accounts for the cost of the wine, which means it pays less Corporation Tax. And because it's classed as remuneration, the NI paid by the company on the benefit-in-kind gets tax relief too, leaving more money left in the company for you to take at a later date.

15.3. EXAMPLE

Let's say you're a member of a wine club that entitles you to a case of wine each month for a monthly subscription of £100. This is the level of additional salary you would require after tax and NI has been deducted by the company. We can now compare the relative tax positions if the £1,200 annual cost is treated as net salary or a benefit-in-kind.

15.3.1. You

	22% TAXPAYER	40% TAXPAYER
Tax on salary £1,200 (x 33 / 67) or (x 41 / 59)	591	834
Tax on benefits of £1,200	264	480
Saving	**327**	**354**

15.3.2. Your company and NI

	22% TAXPAYER	40% TAXPAYER
NI on salary	229	260
NI on benefits	154	154
Saving	**75**	**106**

15.3.3. Corporation Tax saving on a benefit

	40% TAXPAYER
Corporation Tax on annual subscription (£1,200 @ 19%)	228
Corporation Tax on NI (£154 @ 19%)	29
Saving	**257**

15.4. THE PAPERWORK

By taking the following steps you will be making sure that there is no room for a challenge by the Taxman. And with all the paperwork completed correctly there should be no risk of penalties arising at a later date either.

15.4.1. The board minute

Remember any expense charged in the company's accounts has to meet the "wholly and exclusively" test that we talked about earlier. Getting a formal board minute drawn up demonstrates to the Taxman that the benefit was agreed on by the company as a way of rewarding you for your services to the company. There is no need for any special wording, just a statement of the facts as a record for future reference.

Example

The following can be used as an example:

"Meeting of the Board of Directors of XYZ Limited on.... at...

It was resolved that the company approve the payment of Mr X's monthly subscription to..... Wine Club as part of his remuneration package.

This award has been made in recognition of his continuing contribution to the success of the company.

Signed....... company secretary."

Tɪᴘ. Write to your advisor telling him what you're doing so that it can be included on your P11D.

15.4.2. Your contract of employment

Because this is a variation of your remuneration package you will need to incorporate it into your contract of employment by way of an addendum to the main contract.

Example

An example could read: "as of .... the company will pay your subscriptions to ....Wine Club subject to the availability of funds. This benefit-in-kind is to be treated as part of your remuneration package with the company."

15.4.3. Contract with/invoice from the supplier

Getting the wine merchant to invoice the company will make it absolutely clear that the liability for payment belongs with the company and not you.

15.4.4. On the VAT return

As the contract is with the company any VAT charged by the wine club can be reclaimed on your VAT return.

15.4.5. On your P11D

The value of the benefit-in-kind to be included is the contracted value of the subscription before the deduction of VAT.

15.4.6. In the company's accounts

Although there are no special disclosure requirements, if you include the charge for the subscription within "remuneration costs", it reinforces your position that it's part of your overall package.

15.4.7. Your tax return

Simply transfer the value from your P11D to the relevant boxes on your tax return's employment pages. Any tax due will then be collected in the normal way.

15.5. LOW, MEDIUM AND HIGH-RISK STRATEGIES

15.5.1. Low-risk

If you get the paperwork right the low-risk strategy is the one outlined above.

15.5.2. Medium-risk

The company does not get a tax deduction for the costs of the wine because the Taxman doesn't accept that this expense is "wholly and exclusively" for the purpose of the company's trade. This would be the case if it wasn't clear that this was part of your remuneration package.

15.5.3. High-risk

A high-risk strategy here would be to pay the wine club subscriptions without declaring anything to the Taxman. You will get away with paying no tax on the benefits and having the tax relief on the subscription. However, if discovered, the Taxman will hit the company with a bill for the tax and NI on the net benefits grossed up to the "salary" value. In addition, there will be the company's NI bill, plus fines for incorrect P11Ds and interest for late payment. This is because it will be deemed that the company has met a personal liability of the employee.

16. Company plane (or yacht)

16.1. THE EXPENSE

Many of us are frustrated jet setters. We would love, but can't afford, to own and run a yacht or private plane. Is there a way that a company could pay for this instead?

Here, we'll concentrate on a company plane but the Taxman's view is broadly the same for boats. If your existing company just bought an aircraft and you had sole/exclusive use of it then you would be taxed on a benefit-in-kind calculated at 20% of the annual "value" of that plane. This will be calculated by the Inspector as *"total flying hours x the most expensive commercial hire rate"* he can find. So what you should do is...

Step 1. Purchase a light aircraft via a limited company (specifically formed for that purpose) of which you are the sole director/shareholder, using a mortgage secured on the aircraft. Then...

Step 2. Hire out the aircraft to commercial operators - who will use it for commercial operations such as training. Why do this? You are telling the Taxman that the company's objective is to hire out the plane commercially in order to repay the borrowings. It's not a hobby!

TIP. For the benefit of the Taxman prepare some figures showing expected (monthly) cash flows in and out to support your intentions. This should show that the company can repay the mortgage and make a modest profit right from the outset.

Step 3. Draft an agreement between yourself (as a director) and the company specifying that you can only use it on a commercial basis at an agreed rate per hour.

You now don't have exclusive use of the plane, so the Taxman can't use his figures. Instead you agree with him some form of (lower) hourly rate for private use. So how is this done?

The hourly rate for private use could be *"total expenses x number of hours flown by you/total hours"*. Total expenses will be your company's accounts at the end of the year. The name of the game here is to maximise total hours. Total hours will include; **(1)** earning time - hours flown by the customers; **(2)** private use - hours flown by you for pleasure; **(3)** positioning and exercise - flights to place the aircraft where it is needed for hiring or just to turn the engine and prevent static decay; **(4)** servicing - hours in the workshop; and **(5)** idle time - aircraft fully available but unused.

Go to the Taxman with the rate you have calculated and get it agreed before you have to put it on the P11D. This way you avoid any penalties.

TIP. Charge your other business a fee for using the plane as transport for business trips. Increasingly, planes are used for business trips by busy executives in place of our choked road system. What the Taxman can't do is disallow expenses in your other company on the grounds that you have not taken the cheapest transport option.

Don't think that our advice is limited to planes. Anything that you are interested in can be treated in the same way - if it could be hired out commercially. So why not sign up for that course of flying or sailing lessons? Clever tax treatment of what you are doing could help turn your dreams into reality.

16.2. WHAT ARE THE POTENTIAL TAX SAVINGS?

If you buy and run a plane with your own resources then they're likely to have come from income that has already suffered tax. If it's income from your company, this money has probably been extracted as either salary or dividends. If you can reduce your tax bill by getting the company to pay direct then you are in a winning situation. So what are the potential tax savings?

The savings come from establishing that the opportunity with the plane is a business not a personal hobby. The way of getting business status for a plane would be to set up a chartering company. The fact that it might be chartered on occasion to you, as the business owner, shouldn't prevent this, provided you are not the only charterer. If you are going to go down this road, make sure you can demonstrate that you are adopting a 100% business-like approach to the purchase. Ideally you should create and document a fully worked out business plan, and you should be able to demonstrate that you have tried as hard as you can to secure charters.

If the plane is acquired on finance, business treatment enables you to claim the interest element of the finance against tax.

If you are using the plane as the fixed asset of a business, capital allowances are available against the income from the business activity. Capital allowances are the tax equivalent of depreciation and are designed, over the life of the asset, to write off all of its cost against income.

Benefit-in-kind trap

Example

You manage to find third party charters for the company plane for 20 weeks of the year, and use it yourself for three weeks. Instead of what you would probably regard as fair, that is a benefit-in-kind charge of 3/23 of the cost of providing the plane, you could end up with 32/52 of the costs as a benefit, on the basis that, all the time it was not being chartered by others, it was "available" for your use.

TIP. Establish that the plane is not available to you at times when you are not using it. A board minute and actual use that complies with it should be effective in reducing the benefit-in-kind charge.

16.3. THE PAPERWORK

As we have said already the tax advantages depend on being able to successfully claim some kind of "business" status for the plane.

If you only want that plane for private use, how can you pretend that it is a business asset? Well, there is certainly no question of pretending anything; valid tax planning has to be on the basis of full disclosure and none of our advice depends on deceiving the Taxman or anyone else.

16.3.1. Projected cash flow and profit and loss

Prepare some figures showing expected (monthly) cash flows in and out to support your intentions. This should show that the company can fund any loan secured on the plane and make a modest profit right from the outset.

16.3.2. Agreement between you and the company

Have a formal written agreement between yourself and the company specifying that you can only use the plane on a commercial basis at an agreed rate per hour.

16.3.3. The board minute

Have a board minute on file agreeing to your use of the plane but on a restricted basis.

You're not trying to hide anything from the Taxman; in fact you want this out in the open and agreed.

16.3.4. On your P11D

If the hourly rate for private use per your agreement with the company is *"total expenses x number of hours flown by you/ total hours"* you will need a record on your P11D file of **(1)** An analysis of the planes total costs (including VAT); and **(2)** Total hours, broken down into the components outlined above (from the plane's own log book).

Your company then needs to enter the value of *"private hours x agreed rate per hour"* in the tax year on your P11D.

16.3.5. Your tax return

You simply take the figure given to you by the company for your P11D benefit and put it on your tax return. No further disclosures are required by you.

16.4. LOW, MEDIUM AND HIGH-RISK STRATEGIES

16.4.1. Low-risk

If you get the paperwork right the low-risk strategy is the one outlined above.

So why not sign up for that course of flying or sailing lessons and make a note of the date of the next boat show? Clever tax treatment of what you are doing could help turn your dreams into reality.

16.4.2. Medium-risk

You forget to draft an agreement between yourself and the company specifying that you can only use it on a commercial basis at an agreed rate per hour. If the Taxman asks for a copy of the agreement and you can't produce one he'll tax you on the plane being available to you for the whole year! Ouch.

You now don't have exclusive use of the plane, so the Taxman can't assess you with a full year's benefit-in-kind.

16.4.3. High-risk

You don't bother with a separate company and buy it with funds in your existing business. There's no real prospect of external chartering, no agreement between you and your company and it ends up being your exclusive plane. The Taxman picks out this large addition to fixed assets and opens an enquiry into all aspects of your existing company's affairs not just the plane perk! Or you get lucky and he doesn't spot anything for six years.

17. Gym membership

17.1. THE EXPENSE

If the company meets the personal expenditure of a director or employee, the Taxman can assess the company to tax on the difference between the sum paid out and the gross salary equivalent. He'll also want NI and penalties on top. So how is it that you can get your gym membership paid for by the company without being penalised in this way and what are the savings that can be made?

17.2. WHAT ARE THE POTENTIAL TAX SAVINGS?

If you pay for your membership yourself it will come from income that's already had tax deducted from it. However, if the company pays then you save some of the tax that you would have paid on that income withdrawal. The potential savings are examined below.

17.2.1. Savings on your salary

If the company pays for your membership fees it will be treated as a benefit-in-kind and taxable on you as the director/employee, based on the amount paid.

The tax on this will be less than the amount you would have had to take in salary to pay your membership. In addition, there won't be any employees' NI to pay either. The company will pay NI, but once again it will be on a lesser amount than the salary equivalent.

17.2.2. Corporation Tax

Your company will get a tax deduction for all the cost of the gym membership. In addition, the NI paid by the company on the value of the benefit-in-kind gets tax relief. This means there's more money left in the company for you to take at a later date.

17.3. EXAMPLE

Let's say your annual gym membership fees for you and your family are £1,500. This is the amount you would need after tax and NI has been deducted by the company. We can now compare the relative tax positions if the £1,500 is treated as net salary or a benefit-in-kind.

17.3.1. You

	22% TAXPAYER	40% TAXPAYER
Tax on salary £1,500 (x 33 / 67) or (x 41 / 59)	739	1,042
Tax on benefits of £1,500	330	600
Saving	**409**	**442**

17.3.2. Your company and NI

	22% TAXPAYER	40% TAXPAYER
NI on salary @12.8%	287	325
NI on benefits @12.8%	192	192
Saving	**95**	**133**

17.3.3. Corporation Tax saving on a benefit

	40% TAXPAYER
Corporation Tax on annual subscription (£1,500 @ 19%)	285
Corporation Tax on NI (£192 @ 19%)	36
Saving	**321**

17.4. THE PAPERWORK

By taking the following steps you will be making sure that there is no room for a challenge by the Taxman. And with all the paperwork done correctly there should be no risk of penalties arising at a later date either.

17.4.1. The board minute

Remember any expense charged in the company's accounts has to meet the "wholly and exclusively" test. Getting a formal board minute drawn up demonstrates to the Taxman that the benefit was agreed on by the company as a way of rewarding you for your services to the company. There is no need for any special wording, just a statement of the facts as a record for future reference.

Example

"Meeting of the Board of Directors of XYZ Limited on.... at...

It was resolved that the company approve the payment of an annual subscription to .... as part of their remuneration package.

This award has been made in recognition of their continuing contribution to the success of the company.

Signed....... company secretary."

17.4.2. Contract of employment

Because this is a variation of your remuneration package you will need to incorporate it into your contract of employment by way of an addendum.

Example

"as of .... the company will pay your membership of .... This benefit-in-kind is to be treated as part of your remuneration package with the company."

17.4.3. Contract with/invoice from the supplier

Getting the supplier to invoice the company will make it absolutely clear that the liability for payment belongs with the company and not you.

17.4.4. On the VAT return

As the contract is with the company, any VAT charged on the membership fees can be reclaimed on your company's VAT return.

17.4.5. On your P11D

The value of the benefit-in-kind to be included is the total cost of the membership before the deduction of VAT.

17.4.6. In the company's accounts

Although there are no special disclosure requirements, if you include the charge for the cost of the gym membership as part of "remuneration costs" it reinforces your position that it's part of your pay package.

17.4.7. On your tax return

Simply transfer the values from your P11D to the relevant boxes on your tax return's employment pages. Any tax due will then be collected in the normal way.

17.5. LOW, MEDIUM AND HIGH-RISK STRATEGIES

17.5.1. Low-risk

Getting the paperwork right as described above cuts all risk down to an absolute minimum.

17.5.2. Medium-risk

If it's unclear that the payment is part of your remuneration package there's a risk that the company won't be allowed a deduction in the accounts under the "true and fair" rules. This means a loss of Corporation Tax relief.

17.5.3. High-risk

A high-risk strategy here would be for your company to pay for your gym membership without declaring any benefit to you personally. However, if discovered, the Taxman will hit the company with a bill for the tax and NI on the payment grossed up to the "salary" value because the company has met a personal liability of the employee.

18. Garage storage

18.1. THE EXPENSE

A colleague has told you that they charge their company rent for the use of their garage - presumably just to keep their company car in out of the rain. What's the full story here and is this really something you could take advantage of?

The Taxman say's that any allowance paid to an employee for keeping a company vehicle in the employee's own garage will be taxable. In such a case, PAYE needs to be applied - meaning the payment is treated as net salary and then grossed up to work out the tax and NI due. This applies whether or not the garage is attached to your residence. So it doesn't look as if your colleague is telling the full story. However, there are a couple of loopholes that you might be able to exploit.

Protecting the company car

The Taxman's manual refers to circumstances in which the employer requires the employee to rent a garage for a vehicle owned by the employer and accepts that there is no benefit to the employee in these circumstances, even if the cost of renting the garage is paid by the employee and reimbursed by the employer.

> *Example*
>
> *David's house has no garage, so consequently, cars are parked on the road. A garage recently became available nearby and he arranged for the company to rent this and the car is now kept there overnight and during other periods when it is not being used.*

There is no specification as to how much rent you are allowed to claim or how big (other than car size) the garage should be. Just don't go over the top. The key thing is that you must not own the garage.

Storeroom, not garage

Let's say, for example, that you use your garage to store product samples for your company. Is it possible to claim some expenses in addition to the rent claimed for using your home as an office?

You'll always need to work hard to convince the Taxman on anything to do with your home. But if you use part of your home for the duties of your employment (for example, because you live and work some distance from your head office), you can claim the additional cost of working from home. If you have a home working agreement with your company in place, it can pay you a minimum of £2 a week tax-free to cover these additional costs. However, any allowance paid to you for use of your garage normally counts as earnings. Therefore PAYE should be applied to the payment. This will be the case whether or not the garage is attached to your home.

However, where an employer claims that the payment to an employee is rent chargeable on the employee as property income, then this is tax deductible for the company and not earnings of the employee. So all you need to do is charge your company rent for the use of your garage.

18.2. THE PAPERWORK

By taking the following steps you will be making sure that there is no room for a challenge by the Taxman. And with all the paperwork completed correctly there should be no risk of penalties arising at a later date either.

Protecting the company car

Get a letter from your company insisting that the car is locked in a garage overnight "for security reasons". There should also be reference in the letter to the fact that you will be reimbursed for the additional costs involved in this garaging.

The company should also approach its tax office to inform the Taxman why it considers no entry on a P11D is needed for this specific expense payment and requesting agreement to this. It's easier to get this agreed right from the start rather than several years later during a routine PAYE inspection visit.

Storeroom, not garage

Alternatively, record any payment to you by your company for use of your garage as rent, both in your company's books as an expense and on your own tax return as income. However, on your return you now get to claim for any additional costs of meeting your company's requirements for the safe keeping etc. of that stock whilst it's in your garage.

18.2.1. Rental agreement

Back up this storeroom payment with a licence agreement between you and your company setting out the terms and conditions of the rental agreement. Include the additional measures your company expects you to take over preserving the condition of the stock.

Example

- *The property owners to take such steps as are necessary for the items stored not to be exposed to high or low temperatures whilst within the garage storage*

- *The property owners to put suitable security and fire prevention measures in place to reduce the risk of loss of items held in the garage storage*

- *The property owners to put such procedures in place that will allow the garage storage to comply with the Company's health and safety policy.*

18.2.2. On the VAT return

There's no VAT involved in this expense.

18.2.3. On your P11D

No entry required.

18.2.4. In the company's accounts

Although there are no special disclosure requirements, if you include the payment for rent under "rent and rates" it reinforces your position that it's that type of business expense.

18.2.5. On your tax return

You'll need to record the rent you receive from your company as rental income on your tax return. Remember to claim the costs of supplying this facility to your company (in line with any specific requirements it might have).

18.3. LOW, MEDIUM AND HIGH-RISK STRATEGIES

18.3.1. Low-risk

Getting the paperwork right as described above cuts all risk down to an absolute minimum.

Tɪᴘ. As self-employed, if you already claim "use of home as office" include the garage as an additional room for apportioning costs between business and non-business. Plus claim for costs directly related to providing that storage.

18.3.2. Medium-risk

If it's unclear that the payment is rent so there's a risk that it will be treated as net salary and the Taxman will come looking for tax and NI on the gross equivalent.

18.3.3. High-risk

You pay yourself a round sum allowance from the company for the privilege of parking your company car in your own garage. If discovered, the Taxman will want to treat this as net salary that needs grossing up for unpaid Tax and NI. There will also be interest and penalties.

19. Nannies

19.1. THE EXPENSE

Unfortunately, hiring a nanny to provide additional childcare in your own home comes with a tax cost. As a general rule, if an employee such as a nanny earns more than (currently) £89 a week you have to operate a payroll for them. This means working out how much income tax and NI is due on their wages/salary and paying this across to the Taxman on a regular basis.

If you engage a nanny through an agency they would deal with all the PAYE etc. for you. But you would probably end up paying more as the agency builds its own profit margin into the going rate for nannies.

Can't you just put the nanny onto your company's payroll instead of employing them yourself? We don't recommend this, even though it may save on agency fees. The Taxman's view is that the full cost of the nanny's wages plus employers' NI is treated as your extra salary. You can't even offset the tax and NI already paid by the nanny through the payroll against your own surprise tax bill.

Tɪᴘ. Get the contract to supply a nanny made out between your company and the agency not with you as an individual. Go down the route of having this as a benefit-in-kind as part of you overall remuneration package with your company.

19.2. WHAT IT MIGHT COST

19.2.1. If you directly employ a nanny

Example

Nanny is paid £15,000 a year by the Darling family to look after their children. She would be paid less if she lived with the family but she chooses to have her own accommodation (lives out). On top of the salary the family has to pay employers' NI of £1,275.52 pa ((£15,000 - £5,035 NI free) x 12.8%).

From Nanny's salary the Darlings have to deduct a total of £1,096.15 in employees' NI and £1,934.30 in income tax and pay it over to the Taxman - together with the employers' NI. This leaves Nanny with an after tax salary of £11,969.55 (£997.46 per month).

19.2.2. As a benefit-in-kind from your company

Example

Your company engages an agency to provide the nanny as part of your remuneration package. On a cost to the company of £17,625 (£15,000 plus VAT) you, as a 40% taxpayer, will pay income tax of £7,050 - even though the company is able to claim back the VAT through its VAT return. Your company's employers' Class 1A NI bill on this benefit-in-kind is £2,256 (£17,625 x 12.8%). However, the Corporation Tax deduction is worth £3,280 (£15,000 + £2,265 = £17,265 at, say, 19%).

19.3. WHAT ARE THE POTENTIAL TAX SAVINGS?

If you pay the nanny yourself it will come from income that's already had tax deducted from it. However, if the company pays then you save some of the tax that you would have paid on that income withdrawal.

As part of your remuneration package, your company will get a tax deduction for the cost of providing the nanny. You can't claim a tax deduction for the nanny through your own tax return. And this means there's more money left in the company for you to take at a later date.

19.4. THE PAPERWORK

By taking the following steps you will be making sure that there is no room for a challenge by the Taxman. And with all the paperwork completed correctly there should be no risk of penalties arising at a later date either.

19.4.1. The board minute

Remember, any expense charged in the company's accounts has to meet the "wholly and exclusively" test. Getting a formal board minute drawn up demonstrates to the Taxman that the benefit was agreed on by the company as a way of rewarding you for your services to the company. There is no need for any special wording, just a statement of the facts as a record for future reference.

Example

"Meeting of the Board of Directors of XYZ Limited on.... at...

It was resolved that the company approve the engagement of a nanny
(through an agency) as part of ...... 's remuneration package.

This award has been made in recognition of their continuing contribution
to the success of the company.

Signed .... company secretary".

19.4.2. Contract of employment

Because this is a variation of your remuneration package you will
need to incorporate it into your contract of employment by way of
addendum.

Example

"as of .... the company will engage a nanny (through an agency). This
benefit-in-kind is to be treated as part of your remuneration package
with the company."

19.4.3. Contract with/invoice from the supplier

Getting the supplier to invoice the company will make it absolutely clear
that the liability for payment belongs with the company and not you.

19.4.4. On the VAT return

As the contract is with the company, any VAT charged by the nanny's
agency can be reclaimed on your company's VAT return.

19.4.5. On your P11D

The value of the benefit-in-kind to be included is the total cost of the
nanny (including VAT).

19.4.6. In the company's accounts

Although there are no special disclosure requirements, if you include
the charge for the cost of the nanny as part of "remuneration costs" it
reinforces the position that it's part of your pay package.

19.4.7. On your tax return

Simply transfer the values from your P11D to the relevant boxes on your tax return's employment pages. Any tax due will then be collected in the normal way.

19.5. LOW, MEDIUM AND HIGH-RISK STRATEGIES

19.5.1. Low-risk

Getting the paperwork right as described above cuts all risk down to an absolute minimum.

19.5.2. Medium-risk

If it's unclear that the payment is part of your remuneration package there's a risk that the company won't be allowed as a deduction in the accounts under the "true and fair" rules. This means a loss of Corporation Tax relief.

19.5.3. High-risk

A high-risk strategy here would be to use the company bank account to settle what you owe the nanny and not declare the benefit to you on your P11D. You get away with paying no tax on the benefits and your company might initially get tax relief on the cost of the agency nanny. However, if this expense distorts your company's accounts too much this increases the chance of the Taxman opening an enquiry. If the truth is discovered the Taxman will hit the company with a bill for the tax and NI on this expense grossed up as "salary". In addition there will be the company NI bill, plus fines for incorrect P11D's and interest for late payment.

20. Petty cash differences

20.1. THE EXPENSE

The Taxman doesn't like cash because it doesn't give him a nice audit trail to follow. He just assumes that you are up to no good if cash is involved. OK, most business expenses these days are invoiced or settled using a company credit card, but cash floats are still used on certain occasions.

For example, you could be off to see a customer and you will need to meet out-of-pocket expenses. Naturally you take some cash from the petty cash tin, perhaps leaving a note to say how much was taken. In the absence of evidence, the Taxman will see the money as taken "net of tax". Meaning he wants to gross up the petty cash difference for income tax and NI and he will ask you to pay it.

> *Example*
>
> *Paul takes £100 per week from petty cash, a total of £5,200 for the year. He is a 40% taxpayer already paying maximum employees' NI. £5,200 translates into £8,813.55 (£5,200 x 100/59) gross salary. This means that the Taxman collects the difference of £3,613 plus £1,128 in employers' NI, making a total of £4,741. Hardly worth drawing the cash in the first place is it. Or, Paul has to draw dividend from his company to repay the £5,200 before the tax year closes, which will cost him an additional £1,300 (£5,200 x 25%) in income tax. A cheaper solution but it's still painful.*

In practice, you might not be able to get receipts for everything you spend the cash on, e.g. street parking, or just forget to. A large cup of designer coffee in a railway station could cost you as much as £3.00. But who would remember to get a receipt for this? If the Taxman sees you haven't got one, he would still want to tax you on the difference one way or another.

What you need to do is to collect evidence that the missing cost was a business expense. So when returning from your trip try and tie up where the money went. The important thing is to get the record as close as you can.

You could keep a record of where you travelled to, who you saw and what you spent in your diary. However, you probably don't feel comfortable with the Taxman nosing through your appointments etc. Better to record this on a separate sheet of paper, to which you can add a list of expenses matching what's been spent.

Advances for expenses

An advance on account of expenses to be incurred by an employee is strictly a loan for tax purposes. If the total of all loans from your company exceeds £5,000 then you pay tax on a notional interest benefit, calculated at a rate of 5%. However, the Taxman has issued a statement of practice which removes certain advances from this test. The main conditions that need to be satisfied are; **(1)** the maximum amount advanced at any one time must not exceed £1,000; **(2)** advances must be spent within six months; and **(3)** the employee must account for how he has spent the amount advanced. As long as these conditions are met such advances will not be treated as loans.

Euros

From time-to-time a director or employee will have occasion to travel to Euroland on business. Most of the travel and subsistence can be taken care of by the company credit card. However, there is always the need to carry cash "just in case". Indeed cash is a necessity for paying local taxes in some of the member sates. So you have a business need for a reasonable stock of Euros in the same way as you have a need for a petty cash float.

Tip. There is a good argument these days for having a Euro as well as a Sterling petty cash tin. If you personally need to dip into the Euro tin remember to replenish it as soon as possible.

20.2. THE PAPERWORK

By taking the following steps you will be making sure that there is no room for a challenge by the Taxman. And with all the paperwork completed correctly there should be no risk of penalties arising at a later date either.

20.2.1. Your expense claim

Fill out an expense claim. If you have spent some of the money on personal items then record it as such. It's better to pay tax on the small amount taken rather than on the whole cash difference.

TIP. Have a pad of petty cash vouchers or Post-it notes in your briefcase. Use these to note down a variety of minor expenses.

20.2.2. Company policy on overpayments

To help slow the Taxman down on "the difference is additional net salary" line of attack, make sure that the following appears in your company's expenses policy:

"Overpayments remain Company money at all times. They never form part of employees' salary or remuneration packages".

This also gives you the option of making good any overpayments (such as cash differences) within a reasonable period of them being discovered.

20.2.3. On the VAT return

In order to recover the VAT you are charged you should obtain a VAT invoice, although for supplies of less than £250 excluding VAT you only need a less detailed tax invoice. Valid VAT receipts (with a VAT number) are needed to claim back VAT on your expenses. However, by concession, there are some minor items that you don't have to have a receipt for. The supply of taxi services is a taxable supply but most self-employed taxi drivers are not VAT registered, so when you get a receipt for your expenses claim ask the taxi driver if he has charged VAT.

20.2.4. On your P11D

These are not reimbursed expenses so they don't need to be disclosed on your P11D or covered by a dispensation from the Taxman.

20.2.5. In the company's accounts

Any remaining petty cash differences from your cash withdrawals will be booked by your accountant as a reduction to your director's loan account, to be cleared by additional salary or dividend before the accounts are signed off for that year.

20.2.6. Your tax return

No additional entries are required. This should all have been taken care of through the other entries on your return.

20.3. LOW, MEDIUM AND HIGH-RISK STRATEGIES

20.3.1. Low-risk

If you get the paperwork right the low-risk strategy is the one outlined above.

20.3.2. Medium-risk

The company does not get a tax deduction for your missing expenses because the Taxman doesn't accept that these expenses were "wholly and exclusively" for the purpose of the company's trade.

In the absence of expense claims the Taxman will be happy to include any unresolved petty cash differences as net salary from your company.

20.3.3. High-risk

You do nothing about your petty cash differences.

However, you won't have to wait for an enquiry before you have to deal with this, your accountant will have to make a decision about this "cash difference" when preparing your accounts or P11Ds.

21. The weekend away

21.1. THE EXPENSE

Getting away from work for any reasonable length of time can be difficult. If you fancy a weekend or two away, are there ways that you can legitimately get your company to pay for them?

As a general rule, transportation costs are tax deductible if the primary purpose of your trip is business-related. So how can you take advantage of this? Say you would like to travel to the Lake District, primarily to see customers, prospects, suppliers etc. in the area. Or you're due to travel to a conference. Why not squeeze in a couple of extra days to your itinerary to get the break you deserve?

If you have business meetings on, say, Friday and Monday in a particular area, there's no need to go home for the weekend. You can spend Saturday and Sunday at, say, the nearest health spa, tennis club or cricket ground and still get a tax deduction for most of the expenses.

If you travel outside the UK you can write off 100% of your transportation costs if your trip was primarily for business and you were outside the UK for, say, a week or less. On longer foreign trips, the Taxman will look for a business (yes) versus pleasure (no) allocation of expenses.

Investigate where conferences for your industry or profession are being held. See if these coincide with your choice of a nice location for a weekend break, or even just a hotel that has it all. The trip must be seen to be primarily for business for your travel expenses to be deductible along with most, if not all, of your hotel bills.

Your company can claim a full tax deduction for the cost of genuine business travel, related hotel accommodation and subsistence. However, there is a condition - the costs must be incurred "wholly exclusively and necessarily for the furtherance of the trade". So with our weekend break plan, your travel and accommodation costs should be deductible - what you choose to do in the hours when not attending clients is none of the Taxman's business.

Example

You take a four-day business trip. After four days of work-related appointments, you spend two days at the same hotel, swimming and sightseeing. Because you devoted more time to business than pleasure, your travel will be deductible. Other outlays (hotels, meals etc.) may be written off by your company for the business related portion of the trip.

Tip. Keep a log to show that the key days were focused on business. Retain copies of pre-trip correspondence arranging meetings, agendas for the conference, and post-trip follow-ups.

Companion

For you to deduct the travel costs of a spouse or significant other, your companion must be an employee of the company, with a business purpose for going along. However, even if your companion has no business purpose for being there, their attendance doesn't disqualify your business trip. Of course if they meet their own (additional) expenses then there's no real tax issue here. If their bills end up on your company credit card the best way to solve this is to write the company a personal cheque to cover them.

Finally, any of the expenses incurred by your spouse/partner will be deductible if you incur them yourself and just share the benefits with them, e.g. taxi fares, car rental etc.

21.2. WHAT ARE THE POTENTIAL TAX SAVINGS?

If you pay for the whole trip yourself it will come from income that's already had tax deducted from it. However, if the company pays then you save some of the tax that you would have paid on that income withdrawal.

Your company will be permitted to make a deduction in its accounts for the business element of the trip, which means it pays less Corporation Tax.

21.3. THE PAPERWORK

By taking the following steps you will be making sure that there is no room for a challenge by the Taxman. And with all the paperwork done correctly there should be no risk of penalties arising at a later date either.

21.3.1. The board minute

Remember any expense charged in the company's accounts has to meet the "wholly and exclusively" test. Getting a formal board minute drawn up demonstrates to the Taxman that the trip was agreed on by the company for a commercial reason. There is no need for any special wording, just a statement of the facts as a record for future reference.

> *Example*
>
> *A director decided to take an extended trip to visit suppliers, and to take his wife, Jeanette, with him. Before booking the tickets, he called a board meeting at which it was resolved that "Jeanette be asked to accompany John in order to assist him at social engagements for the benefit of the company's business". The company secretary (who just happens to be Jeanette) also recorded in the minutes that the board thought that her presence produced minimal additional expenditure.*

21.3.2. Invoices

Hotel bills etc. should be addressed to the company rather than yourself. In fact, it's probably best to get as much of the trip paid for via the company credit/debit card as possible.

21.3.3. On the VAT return

You can make a reasonable apportionment of VAT between business and non-business purposes if the expenses include a private element.

21.3.4. On your P11D

There will be no entries on your P11D for this trip if you reimburse any private element to the expenses.

21.3.5. In the company's accounts

There are no special disclosure requirements, just include the costs of the trip within "travel costs".

21.3.6. Your tax return

Simply transfer the values from your P11D to the relevant boxes on your tax return's employment pages. Any tax due will then be collected in the normal way.

21.4. LOW, MEDIUM AND HIGH-RISK STRATEGIES

21.4.1. Low-risk

If you get the paperwork right the low-risk strategy is the one outlined above. Add holiday days to a business trip, as practically all costs associated with making that trip are tax deductible. Remember to make a contribution to the resultant company credit card bill for the non-business element.

21.4.2. Medium-risk

The company does not get a tax deduction for the trip because the Taxman doesn't accept that this expense is "wholly and exclusively" for the purpose of the company's trade. This would be the case if it wasn't clear that you had reimbursed the company for any private costs and that the private benefit from the trip as a whole was merely incidental.

21.4.3. High-risk

A high-risk strategy here would be to get the company to pay for the whole cost of the trip without declaring any private element to the Taxman. You will get away with paying no tax on the benefits and your company having the tax relief on the costs. However, if discovered, the Taxman will hit the company with a bill for the tax and NI on private expenses. In addition, the company will have fines for incorrect returns and interest for late payment of tax underpaid. This is because it will be deemed that the company has met a personal liability of an employee.

22. Domestic help

22.1. THE EXPENSE

You're so busy with your company that some of those domestic household chores aren't getting done as regularly as they might be. So paying for someone to come in and help with the cleaning, ironing, etc. is a serious option. It occurs to you that as it's your business that's keeping you occupied why can't it pay for this extra domestic help?

22.2. WHAT IT MIGHT COST

Example

Your company pays £40 every fortnight for two 1½ hour cleaning sessions a week at your home. It uses a firm which provides the cleaning materials etc. and also has insurance cover for their staff whilst in your home including accidental damage clauses. It pays that firm's invoice rather than give you cash to leave for the cleaning staff.

22.3. WHAT ARE THE POTENTIAL TAX SAVINGS?

If you pay for the domestic help out of your own pocket then it's likely to be from income that has already suffered tax. If it's income from your company, this money has probably been extracted as either salary or dividends. If you can reduce your tax bill by getting the company to pay direct then you are in a winning situation.

22.4. THE PAPERWORK

You've reassessed your remuneration package to include a domestic help expense you would like the company to incur as a benefit-in-kind. What your company needs to do is put this arrangement in writing - both amongst the company board minutes and as an addition to your contract of employment.

Once the domestic help has been completed your company then has to get its external reporting right, first to the VATman, then in its accounts and finally to the Taxman on its P11D.

22.4.1. The board minute

If you go down the benefit-in-kind route your company's board minutes should include a commercial reason for the company agreeing to include domestic cleaning arrangements as part of your remuneration package.

Example

The board minute covering domestic help in Jim's home reads as follows: "In recognition of your contribution to the company and to spend more time on company business each week, the company has decided that as part of your remuneration package it will contract and pay for domestic help for two mornings a week at your principal private residence. This is of course subject to the company having sufficient funds to do so."

You're not trying to hide anything from the Taxman; in fact you want this out in the open and agreed.

Tɪᴘ. Write to your advisor telling him what you're planning on doing so that it can be included on your P11D.

22.4.2. Your contract of employment

Your company needs to put this addition to your remuneration package in writing as an amendment to your contract of employment.

Example

Amendment to contract of employment
As from November 30, 2006, the company will contract and pay for domestic help for two mornings a week at your principal private residence. This benefit-in-kind is from that date part of your remuneration package with the company and will be provided by it subject to the company having sufficient funds to do so.

22.4.3. Contract with/invoice from the supplier

You need the domestic help service to be treated as a benefit-in-kind. As such the contract needs to be negotiated by, addressed to and be clearly a liability of the company.

22.4.4. On the VAT return

Most domestic cleaning outfits don't charge VAT, so nothing to take account of here.

22.4.5. On your P11D

Your company needs to enter on your P11D the cost to it of providing you with domestic help as a benefit-in-kind, during the tax year.

22.4.6. In the company's accounts

Transfer the cost of this work out of "office cleaning costs" and into "staff costs". This reinforces your company's argument that it is part of your remuneration package and hence it can claim a tax deduction for it.

22.4.7. Your tax return

You simply take the figure given to you by the company for your P11D benefit and put it on your tax return. No further disclosures are required by you.

22.5. LOW, MEDIUM AND HIGH-RISK STRATEGIES

22.5.1. Low-risk

If you get the paperwork right the low-risk strategy is the one outlined above.

22.5.2. Medium-risk

The company does not get a tax deduction for the costs of domestic help because the Taxman doesn't accept that this expense is "wholly and exclusively" for the purpose of the company's trade. This would be the case if it wasn't clear that this was part of your remuneration package.

22.5.3. High-risk

Your company enters into one contract with your office cleaning company. Their invoice is made out for one amount that includes work at all locations (including your home).

Since there is only one invoice it's going to be difficult for anyone to decide on the private amount. You wait six years and hope the Taxman doesn't pick this up before then. If he does, there will be the overdue tax, interest and penalties to pay.

23. Taxi fares

23.1. THE EXPENSE

Surely the cost of taxi fares to and from business meetings is allowable against your company profits? Yes. However, the Taxman sometimes asks whether any transport has been provided for the director's ordinary commuting, i.e. taxi fare home.

Paying for your ordinary commuting home to work or vice versa, normally produces a tax charge. It's private not business travel, discloseable on your P11D and so taxable on you - with Class 1A employers' NI for the company.

There is no realistic offsetting claim that you can make on your tax return under the "by reason of my employment" banner. But there is a tax concession you can rely on to potentially get round this occasional problem.

As long as the terms of the concession are met, you do not need to include the cost of the transport in pay for PAYE purposes or show it on the P11D. You don't need to get a specific dispensation from the Taxman either. Employees just leave these payments off their tax return - if satisfied the exemption applies.

The terms of the concession are that; **(1)** you're required to work at least until 9pm; **(2)** this is not a regular requirement; **(3)** no more than 60 such journeys in a tax year; **(4)** public transport has ceased or it's not reasonable to use it; and; **(5)** it must be a taxi, hired car or similar private transport.

Tıp **1.** If you are working late out of choice the concession does not apply. But a memo stating who is to work and until when is enough.

Tıp **2.** Avoid having a regular pattern to these payments. If you work late on the same day each week, then the Taxman says the concession does not apply.

Tıp **3.** If the number of journeys exceeds 60 don't panic, you don't get taxed on the whole lot. If 70 journeys were made then 60 payments would be tax-free and ten taxable.

Tip 4. It's not reasonable to use public transport if the level of availability/reliability of the service at that time of night is bad, resulting in the journey home being much longer than normal. So ask your employees to check out the timetables and prove this point in a note to you.

Warning. If, because of working late, you paid yourself the equivalent of, say, a train fare home, this would be taxable. Always pay yourself the equivalent of the taxi fare home.

Car sharing breaks down

If your spouse or partner who normally shares a car with you to get to work, has to go home early because of a domestic emergency, your company can pay the cost of their journey home. There will be no tax or NI to pay if the circumstances couldn't have been anticipated or planned for.

Tip. If you and your partner share a car to get to work this means your company could pay for either of you to travel home by taxi. Just write "car share, domestic emergency" on the petty cash slip or expenses claim. But don't use this trick too often.

23.2. WHAT ARE THE POTENTIAL TAX SAVINGS?

If you pay for taxi fares out of your own pocket then it's likely that it has come from income that has already suffered tax. If it's income from your company this money has probably been extracted as either salary or dividends. If you can reduce your tax bill by getting the company to pay direct then you are in a winning situation. So what are the potential tax savings?

> *Example*
>
> *Fred stopped his business colleague as he stepped out of a taxi and said "Get a bill with the tip included". The cabbie duly obliged with a bill that totalled £40. It took Fred quite a while afterwards to explain how much this £40 taxi bill was actually worth to his colleague. (1) 19% extra more due to Corporation Tax now saved; (2) 49% saved because it doesn't have to come out of his own tax paid money; (3) 12.8% because your company did not need to pay you as much that week to cover your bills; and (4) 17.5% VAT. Without a doubt the difference "without a bill" and not paid by the company (paid from tax paid earnings) he is probably another £20 worse off - so the cab would have cost £60. And he gets a taxi at least four times a week 200 x £60 = £6,000.*

23.2.1. Corporation Tax

Your company can get a tax deduction for the expenditure itself which leaves more money in the company for you to take out at a later stage. **Rule of thumb.** The company will save Corporation Tax on this expense (net of VAT) at the rate of 19%. You will save employees' NI at the rate of either 11% or 1%.

23.3. THE PAPERWORK

23.3.1 Company policy

It's best to have a company policy covering the use of taxis by employees (including directors). This puts the Taxman on the back foot every time.

> *Example*
>
> *Travel by Taxi.*
>
> *Use of public transport (bus, tube or train etc.) is encouraged and should be used wherever possible for business purposes. However, it is recognised that the use of a taxi may, in the following circumstances, be the most effective mode of transport:*
>
> 1. *where equipment or heavy baggage is being carried*
> 2. *when no public transport is available, especially when traveling early in the morning or late at night*
> 3. *when the claimant is pregnant or has a temporary or permanent disability*
> 4. *where personal or financial security is an issue*
> 5. *when it is important to save time*
> 6. *when in an unfamiliar area and uncertain about public transport.*
>
> *You should obtain an official receipt from the taxi driver to substantiate your subsequent travel expense claim, and you must state clearly on the expense form the reason for use of a taxi.*

23.3.2. On the VAT return

In order to recover any VAT you are charged, you should obtain a VAT invoice, although for supplies of less than £250 excluding VAT you only need a less detailed tax invoice. Valid VAT receipts (with a VAT number) are needed to claim back VAT on your expenses. Although by concession you don't have to have a receipt for items under £25.

The supply of taxi services is a taxable supply but most self-employed taxi drivers are not VAT registered, so when you get a receipt for your expenses claim ask the taxi driver if he has charged VAT.

23.3.3. On your P11D

If these are reimbursed expenses they need to be disclosed on your P11D or covered by a dispensation from the Taxman.

23.3.4. In the company's accounts

No special entries required.

23.3.5. On your tax return

No additional entries required, this should all have been taken care of through the other entries on your return.

23.4. LOW, MEDIUM AND HIGH-RISK STRATEGIES

23.4.1. Low-risk

If, after working late, your company pays for your taxi home you could be creating a tax problem for both of you. However, there is a tax concession you can use to stay out of trouble.

Under certain conditions you can pay for taxi fares home tax-free. But make sure there isn't a regular pattern to these payments and that it would take longer if public transport were used.

If you get the paperwork right the low-risk strategy is the one outlined above.

23.4.2. Medium-risk

The company does not get a tax deduction for the costs of a taxi home because the Taxman doesn't accept that this expense is "wholly and exclusively" for the purpose of the company's trade. This would be the case if it wasn't clear that this was part of agreed company policy.

23.4.3. High-risk

Some people might be tempted to ignore the potential tax problem and just "lose" the expenses under general travel expenses or have an account with a local taxi firm and "lose" this private travel in the overall bill. But if it gets picked up during a PAYE inspection you'll get penalties for an incorrect P11D as well as any underpaid tax and NI to pay.

24. Overnight allowance

24.1. THE EXPENSE

When you go on a business trip, how much do you think you can claim as a tax-free allowance? The Taxman's guidance to employers unequivocally says that cash payments for meals must be subjected to PAYE and NI. So you will, presumably, be charged to tax on everything you are paid by way of an allowance (except to the extent that you can show that it is simply a reimbursement of actual expense incurred).

What's the upper limit for an allowance? The Taxman's own "Film Industry Guidance" notes tell us that where employees in the film industry undertake qualifying travel, employers may pay round-sum meal allowances of amounts varying from £6 for breakfast to £24 for an evening meal. Where overnight accommodation is required anything from £60 to £96 can be paid depending on whether the accommodation is in or out of London and whether or not it includes meals.

Surely the same law applies to film industry employees as to any other, so these £60 to £96 a night allowances must be universally available to all employees? He will normally give a dispensation for a scale rate figure as long as he is satisfied that the calculation of it is based on genuine expenses incurred in the past.

TIP. If he's being a bit stingy with you, use the film industry example to bid up the level of your tax-free allowance.

Staying overnight with friends

When you spend a night away from home whilst on business, you may choose to stay with a friend or relative instead of in a hotel. You may show your gratitude to your host by taking a gift or by paying for an evening meal. Obviously the cost of the gift or meal replaces the hotel expenses, which you would have incurred otherwise. Can you reimburse yourself for this without any adverse tax consequences?

TIP. Have a company policy that pays any employee/director a reasonable overnight allowance for expenses incurred staying with a friend or relative. Get this allowance added to your company's P11D dispensation for travel and subsistence expenses. Tell the Taxman you have an internal control over such expenses where you (or your accountant) randomly checks employee expense claims.

To stop the floodgates opening, the Taxman says in his manual that; *"It is not intended that this allowance should be similar in amount to the expense of staying in a hotel, nor that the allowance should necessarily meet the full cost of a meal for two."* A payment of up to £25 per night is considered to be reasonable by the Taxman, but we would say it depends where you were staying. So some room for manoeuvre here.

24.2. WHAT IT MIGHT COST

Example

Your company pays you an allowance of £500 for your five-day business trip to Dublin (£100 a night). If this isn't covered by a dispensation from the Taxman he could come along in future years and tax this as additional net salary. The income tax and employees' NI bill for that would be £347 (£500/59 x 41) plus employers' NI of £108 (£500/59 x 100 x12.8%). On top of which the Taxman would slap an interest charge for late payment of tax due and a penalty for incorrect reporting.

Personal incidental expenses, for example, personal telephone calls, newspapers, laundry, etc., incurred whilst staying away overnight on company business, must be excluded from the accommodation costs. They should be identified separately on the invoice by the hotel, or if this is not possible, highlighted by the claimant and excluded on the expenses claim.

The maximum amount of incidental overnight expenses that an employer may pay tax-free are:

- £5 per night for overnight stays in the UK
- £10 per night for overnight stays outside the UK.

Warning. If a payment is made that exceeds these limits, the whole of it becomes taxable, not just the excess. However, if you have a policy that requires any employee to pay back any excess, and this repayment is made within a reasonable time, the payment will not be treated as exceeding the tax-free limit.

24.3. WHAT ARE THE POTENTIAL TAX SAVINGS?

If you pay for expenses out of your own pocket then it's likely that this comes from income that has already suffered tax. If it's income from your company this money has probably been extracted as either salary or dividends. If you can reduce your tax bill by getting the company to pay direct then you are in a winning situation.

Your company will get a tax deduction for the expenditure. You would not get a tax deduction for it. This leaves more money in the company for you to take out at a later stage. **Rule of thumb.** The company will save Corporation Tax on this expense (net of VAT) at the rate of 19%.

24.4. THE PAPERWORK

Your company needs to put this overnight allowance arrangement in writing - both amongst the company board minutes and included in the dispensation from the Taxman for paying expenses.

24.4.1. The board minute

In your board minute include a commercial reason for the company agreeing to a specific overnight allowance rate as part of your remuneration package.

Example

The board minute covering a new overnight expenses policy is as follows: "Having reviewed the accounts history of overnight accommodation etc. the company has decided that it will be more administratively convenient to pay an expense allowance of £50 per night. For staying with a friend instead of a hotel or B&B the company will reimburse the employee up to £25 for a gift for their hosts."

You're not trying to hide anything from the Taxman; in fact you want this out in the open and agreed.

Tɪᴘ. Write to your advisor telling him what you're doing so that it can be included on your P11D dispensations from the Taxman.

24.4.2. It's the company's policy

Example

Personal incidental expenses

Personal incidental expenses, for example, personal telephone calls, newspapers, laundry, etc., incurred whilst staying away overnight on Company business, must be excluded from the accommodation costs. They should be identified separately on the invoice by the hotel, or if this is not possible, highlighted by the claimant and excluded on the expenses claim.

Example

Overpayment policy
The Company reserves the right to make deductions from salary where there has been, for whatever reason, an overpayment of expenses. Overpayments will be recovered in accordance with the principles outlined below which apply to all staff employed by the Company. Overpayments remain Company money at all times. They never form part of employees' salary or remuneration packages.

24.4.3. On the VAT return

Keep receipts to the value of the claim.

24.4.4. On your P11D

No entry is required with a dispensation from the Taxman.

24.4.5. In the company's accounts

Book to "travel and subsistence costs".

24.4.6. Your tax return

No entry required.

24.5. LOW, MEDIUM AND HIGH-RISK STRATEGIES

24.5.1. Low-risk

Use the £60 to £96 paid tax-free by the film industry to argue with the Taxman for a sizeable increase in your own tax-free allowances. If you get this dispensation in place, and stick to it, then this is a low-risk strategy for claiming expenses.

Also have a company policy that pays any employee/director a reasonable overnight allowance for expenses incurred staying with a friend or relative. Get it added to your P11D dispensations.

24.5.2. Medium-risk

The company does not get a tax deduction for the costs of overnight stays because the Taxman doesn't accept that this expense is "wholly and exclusively" for the purpose of the company's trade.

24.5.3. High-risk

You pay yourself a round sum allowance every time you go on a trip. But you don't bother to get a dispensation covering this from the Taxman, but it gets left off your P11D. You wait six years and hope the Taxman doesn't pick this up before then. If he does, there will be the overdue tax, interest and penalties to pay.

25. Use of the company villa

25.1. THE EXPENSE

Let's say your company decides to invest in holiday property, the main purpose being to reward key customers with free accommodation. It would need to specify the days the customer can have and (to save on your costs) make it clear they have to arrange their own transport, flights etc. The property is then available for you to use personally at other times.

The full annual running costs of the property would be deductible against the profits of the company if it actually benefits the business, i.e. through increased sales. So it would need to keep records of who uses the accommodation and when. Relate this to individual sales and you can easily show the Taxman how the business has benefited from owning the property.

Although your company doesn't get annual tax allowances on the cost of the property itself, the original cost is tax deductible when your company comes to sell the accommodation. Any taxable profit on the sale would be subject to Corporation Tax.

Location

Does the Taxman mind where the company has this property? He would be suspicious at first of a holiday villa in, say, Spain. But Mr Taxman, to make the offer attractive there is no point in having one week in a cottage in Cornwall - most people would want the same week during the summer when it stops raining. So that is why the company owns a villa in Spain. There is also the ready availability of cheap flights to Spain that make it an attractive destination for customers.

Own use

You can use the accommodation yourself but there is a tax cost to this. Even if you or your fellow directors only use, for example, a company villa for a couple of weeks a year, the Taxman will try and say that it is available to you for the whole year and tax you on its annual value.

Tɪᴘ. Have a policy of restricting the use of the villa to a maximum number of weeks for each director. Document these restrictions in board minutes and letters to the directors. Then back this up with a record of when the visits occurred. This will not eliminate the taxable benefit but will severely restrict the Taxman's ability to assess you for tax on it.

25.2. WHAT IT MIGHT COST

If your existing company just bought a villa and you had sole/exclusive use of it then you would be taxed on a benefit-in-kind calculated at 20% of the annual "value" of that accommodation. This will be calculated by the Taxman as the most expensive value he can find.

> *Example*
>
> *Customers occupy the company villa in Spain for 30 weeks of the year, but you use it yourself for three weeks. Instead of what you would probably regard as fair, that is a benefit-in-kind charge of 3/33 thirds of the cost of providing the accommodation, you could end up with 22/52 of the cost as a benefit, on the basis that all the time it was not being occupied by customers, it was "available" for your use.*
>
> *You pay income tax (but no NI) and your company pays employers' class 1A NI on the value of the benefit-in-kind.*

Your company has to calculate the annual value of free accommodation. The calculation of this depends on the type of property as follows:

PROPERTY	CASH EQUIVALENT VALUE
Cost less than £75,000	Gross rateable value
Cost more than £75,000	Gross rateable value plus nominal rent
Situated overseas irrespective of cost	Local market rent
Is rented by the company	Rent paid by the company
Is owned by a person connected with you and rented by the company	Market rent irrespective of the actual rent paid.

You will also be taxable on a proportion of the other costs paid by the employer, e.g. telephone bills, use of furniture, appliances and repairs, internal decoration, heating, lighting and cleaning.

25.3. WHAT ARE THE POTENTIAL TAX SAVINGS?

If you pay for holiday accommodation out of your own pocket then it's likely that this comes out of income that has already suffered tax. If it's income from your company, this money has probably been extracted as either salary or dividends. If you can reduce your tax bill by using company accommodation then you are in a winning situation.

25.4. THE PAPERWORK

If you only want that accommodation for private use, how can you pretend that it is a business asset? Well, there's certainly no question of pretending anything, valid tax planning has to be on the basis of full disclosure and none of our advice depends on deceiving the Taxman or anyone else.

To help obtain a tax deduction for the running costs of the accommodation, what your company needs to do is record its commercial intentions right from the beginning.

It also needs to restrict the potential tax charge on you for private use of the accommodation by limiting its availability to you.

25.4.1. The board minute

The board minute covering the company's decision to acquire holiday accommodation reads as follows:

Example

"The company has decided to invest in holiday accommodation, with the main purpose of offering this free-of-charge to customers as part of specific sales promotion campaigns. The company will retain tight control over the days the customer can have and make it clear that they have to arrange their own transport to and from the accommodation, e.g. flights. It's not the intention to use the accommodation for the provision of hospitality or entertainment generally to customers".

You're not trying to hide anything from the Taxman; in fact you want this out in the open and agreed.

25.4.2. Marketing campaign

The full annual running costs of the property would be deductible against the profits of the company if it actually benefits the business. So keep copies of any marketing material you regularly produce using the availability of the accommodation as an incentive to lift sales.

Tɪᴘ. Keep records of who and when customers use the accommodation. Relate this to individual sales and you can easily show the Taxman how the business has benefited from owning the property.

25.4.3. Agreement with the company

Draft an agreement between yourself (the director) and the company specifying that you can only use the accommodation for a fixed number of weeks each year.

> *Example*
>
> *Private use agreement*
>
> *The company ………………………………. [insert company name]*
>
> *The employee ……………………………… [insert employee name]*
>
> *The employee agrees to use the …………………[insert address of holiday accommodation] owned by …………… [insert company name] for no more than ……………… [insert number of] agreed days per year. In total the employee shall only be entitled to use it on ……….. [insert number] occasions per quarter.*
>
> *The Company agrees to favour the employee with ……………………… [insert number of] days for accommodation during the period of this Agreement.*
>
> *Signature of employee...*
>
> *Signed by (on behalf of the company) ....*
>
> *Date of agreement..*
>
> *I .... [insert employee name] confirm that I have read, understood and accept the Terms & Conditions of Hire.*

25.4.4. Contracts with/invoices from suppliers

Contracts with local agents and other service providers for the accommodation need to be negotiated by, addressed to and be clearly a liability of the company (not yours).

25.4.5. Value of the accommodation

If situated overseas, get a local valuer to confirm in writing what rent the company's property would have obtained if it were let on the open market. This carries more weight than simply looking up adverts for property rentals on the Internet.

25.4.6. VAT

The company should be able to claim back any VAT charged on the running costs of the property, but restricted to the proportion of business use of the accommodation.

25.4.7. On your P11D

Your company needs to enter the benefit-in-kind figure for this free accommodation on your P11D.

25.4.8. In the company's accounts

No adjustment required to reflect the value of the benefit-in-kind.

25.4.9. Your tax return

You simply take the figure given to you by the company for your P11D benefit and put it on your tax return. No further disclosures are required by you.

25.5. LOW, MEDIUM AND HIGH-RISK STRATEGIES

25.5.1. Low-risk

If you get the paperwork right the low-risk strategy is the one outlined above.

25.5.2. Medium-risk

The company does not get a tax deduction for the running costs associated with accommodation because the Taxman doesn't accept that this expense is "wholly and exclusively" for the purpose of the company's trade. This would be the case if it wasn't clear that it had been used for business purposes.

25.5.3. High-risk

You only use the accommodation for private purposes and pretend that it is a business asset. Little or no declaration is made for the benefit-in-kind of this private use. You wait six years and hope the Taxman doesn't pick this up before then. If he does, there will be the overdue tax, interest and penalties to pay on the disallowed running costs as well as the value of the benefit-in-kind.

26. Advisors' fees

26.1. THE EXPENSE

Your company probably receives an annual bill with lots of zeros from advisors for their professional services during the year - such as accounts, tax and consultancy. But in amongst all these there could be costs for time spent on your personal tax affairs. Is this really an issue for the Taxman?

26.2. WHAT IT MIGHT COST

Any personal tax work paid for by the company is treated as a benefit-in-kind and so taxable. As a director, any benefit-in-kind you receive from the company has to be included on your annual return of benefits form (P11D) that the company sends to the Taxman.

If you forget to put this benefit on the P11D then (if discovered), the company could be liable for a fine of up to £3,000 for filing an incomplete return (although in practice this is rarely levied). But the company will have to pay employers' NI on the benefit omitted at 12.8% of its value.

As you're viewed as receiving a benefit from the company, you have to pay income tax on the value of this at your highest rate of tax.

But how do you put a value on the completion of your tax return and other personal tax work? If it's not specified on your advisor's bill, then the Taxman would estimate the value, either as; **(1)** an estimated percentage of your advisor's overall bill or; **(2)** an estimate of the number of hours that could have been charged by the most expensive advisor in town (plus VAT).

26.3. WHAT ARE THE POTENTIAL TAX SAVINGS?

If you pay your advisor's fees out of your own pocket then it's likely that this comes out of income that has already suffered tax. If it's income from your company, this money has probably been extracted as either salary or dividends. If you can reduce your tax bill by getting the company to pay direct then you are in a winning situation.

26.4. THE PAPERWORK

You've reassessed your remuneration package to include personal tax return completion you would like the company to incur, as a benefit-in-kind for yourself. What your company needs to do is put this arrangement in writing - both amongst the company board minutes and as an addition to your contract of employment.

26.4.1. The board minute

If you go down the benefit-in-kind route your company's board minutes should include a commercial reason for the company agreeing to include your advisor's fees as part of your remuneration package.

> *Example*
>
> *The board minute covering advisors' fees reads as follows: "In recognition of your contribution to the company and to avoid the distraction of making sure you have paid the right amount of tax, the company has decided that as part of your remuneration package that it will contract and pay for the advisor's fees for completing and submitting your annual personal tax return. This is, of course, subject to the company having sufficient funds to do so. This does not include any premium for fee protection insurance that the advisor may offer you. This must be paid direct by yourself."*

26.4.2. Your contract of employment

Your company needs to put this addition to your remuneration package in writing as an amendment to your contract of employment.

> *Example*
>
> *Amendment to contract of employment*
> *As from November 30, 2006, the company will contract and pay for advisor's fees for completion and submission of your annual personal tax return. This benefit-in-kind is from that date part of your remuneration package with the company and will be provided by it subject to the company having sufficient funds to do so.*

26.4.3. Contract with/invoice from the supplier

You need the advisor's service to be treated as a benefit-in-kind. As such, the contract with them needs to be negotiated by, addressed to and be clearly a liability of the company (not yours).

Tip. Agree a reasonable cost with your advisor for personal tax services. Then obtain a separate invoice addressed to the company for this nominal amount you have agreed. They will probabaly do your personal work at "cost" anyway - as a loss leader to the main company account.

26.4.4. On the VAT return

If your company has been charged VAT by the advisor then it should be able to claim it back via its VAT return.

26.4.5. On your P11D

Your company needs to enter on your P11D the cost to it of providing you with this service from an advisor as a benefit-in-kind (inclusive of VAT), during the tax year.

26.4.6. In the company's accounts

Transfer the cost of this work out of "professional fees" and into "staff costs". This reinforces your company's argument that it is part of your remuneration package and hence it can claim a tax deduction for it.

26.4.7. Your tax return

You simply take the figure given to you by the company for your P11D benefit and put it on your tax return. No further disclosures are required by you.

26.5. LOW, MEDIUM AND HIGH-RISK STRATEGIES

26.5.1. Low-risk

Personal tax services paid for by the company are a taxable benefit. Avoid the Taxman choosing a figure to suit himself by agreeing a nominal figure with your advisor for the work done.

If you get the paperwork right the low-risk strategy is the one outlined above.

26.5.2. Medium-risk

The company doesn't get a tax deduction for part of your advisors' fees because the Taxman doesn't accept that this expense is "wholly and exclusively" for the purpose of the company's trade. This would be the case if it wasn't clear that the company was paying for, say, your personal tax return to be dealt with as part of your remuneration package.

26.5.3. High-risk

You leave the total fee from your advisor in "professional fees" and don't split out any private element.

If the Taxman actually asks *"who pays for your tax return?"* can't you just tell him you did it all yourself? Well you could try this approach. But the Taxman may already have authority from you to deal with your advisor direct on your tax affairs. If he has correspondence on file showing that he has done work for you, your argument would look a little weak. What would stick out like a sore thumb would be if your advisor had used a piece of computer software to produce a return which was not available to you. Or if filled in manually, hadn't it better look like your own handwriting?

The real sting in the tail is that the Taxman can go back up to six years to work out how much NI and tax is owed. With interest on top, this could mean the company ends up facing quite a bill.

27. Parking near work

27.1. THE EXPENSE

The Taxman doesn't allow you to claim the expense of your ordinary commuting to work (including car parking) against your own personal tax. Although you might regard it as necessary in order to be able to turn up for work he doesn't think it's necessary to do your job. A fine distinction indeed but one he has stuck to and won cases with. However, what if the company pays for the parking instead?

If your company were to apply for and pay for a season ticket for parking at or near to work you would not be taxed on the cost of this. There's no employers' NI on this payment and the company gets a Corporation Tax deduction. (Even if you've already paid for a parking permit at or near work, you can be reimbursed tax-free.)

But how near is near? The space doesn't have to be provided in a car park immediately adjacent to or attached to the office, but it must be located within a reasonable distance, to be regarded as "at or near work" by the Taxman.

27.2. WHAT IT MIGHT COST

Example

Let's say that in your local car park you pay £3.00 a day for 230 days (allowing for bank holidays, annual leave of four weeks and sick leave) that's £690 you are out of pocket. That's equivalent to gross salary or bonus from your company of £1,030 (£690/67 x 100) if you're a basic rate taxpayer; for a higher rate taxpayer it's £1,169 (£690/59 x 100) you'll need to be paid before deduction of tax and NI just to able to afford the parking.

27.3. WHAT ARE THE POTENTIAL TAX SAVINGS?

If you pay for parking near work out of your own pocket then it's likely that this comes out of income that has already suffered tax. If it's income from your company this money has probably been extracted as either salary or dividends. If you can reduce your tax bill by getting the company to pay direct then you are in a winning situation.

Once you get to appreciate the potential tax savings that are to be had you might even agree to take your next pay rise in the form of a parking permit rather than cash.

Example

Penny earns £15,000 a year and currently pays £3.00 a day to park her car near the office. This costs her £690 a year out of her taxed income. If Penny forgoes a 3% pay increase (£15,000 x 3% = £450) in return for free parking which costs the company £450 (with a discount for a paying in advance) on an annual season ticket, the savings are as follows:

	£	£
Cost saved on parking		690.00
3% pay rise sacrificed (*)	450.00	
Tax at 27% on £450	(99.00)	
NI at 11% £450	(49.50)	
Net pay forgone		301.50
Net savings		**388.50**

(*) The employer saves NI at 12.8% on the cost of the season ticket instead of paying salary.

27.4. THE PAPERWORK

27.4.1. Parking permit

Get your company to apply and pay for a season ticket for parking at or near to work, and you will not be taxed on the cost of this.

27.4.2. Salary sacrifice

Any agreement to replace salary or a pay rise with a free parking permit must be made in advance of the pay rise taking effect on that salary. If substitution is made in arrears the Taxman will ignore the reduction in the cash salary and continue to tax the original gross salary amount.

27.4.3. On your P11D

Your company doesn't need to enter anything on your P11D.

27.4.4. In the company's accounts

Leave the cost of this parking within, say, "motor expenses".

27.4.5. Your tax return

There is nothing for you to enter on your personal tax return.

27.5. LOW, MEDIUM AND HIGH-RISK STRATEGIES

27.5.1. Low-risk

If your company pays in advance for parking at or near your workplace the cost of this is free of tax and NI (for both of you). Indeed, taken as a substitute for salary this could save both even more tax. Of course you need to get the paperwork right up front.

27.5.2. Medium-risk

Any agreement to replace salary or a pay rise with a free parking permit must be made in advance of the pay rise taking effect on that salary. If substitution is made in arrears the Taxman will ignore the reduction in the cash salary and continue to tax the original gross salary amount.

27.5.3. High-risk

The parking near work turns out to be parking somewhere else e.g. for a railway station car park or even near your flat in town! The real sting in the tail here is that the Taxman can go back up to six years to work out how much NI and tax is owed. With interest on top, this could mean the company ends up facing quite a bill for this misinterpretation of the rules.

28. Entertaining

28.1. THE EXPENSE

The cost of entertaining is not a deductible expense for tax purposes either for you or your company, so it's important to know what's classed as entertainment.

Business entertainment includes hospitality of any kind (for example, meals, parties, hospitality tents at sporting events) provided by you or a member of your staff, in connection with your business. It doesn't include anything provided for members of staff, except where the provision of entertainment for the staff is incidental to its provision for clients. This means that a staff party won't come under these rules, but a member of staff attending an event for clients will.

28.1.1 Customers

If you provide customers with free food, drinks, or tickets to, e.g. the rugby, the Taxman says you must exclude the full cost of the event from your accounts, so you don't get tax relief on anything that involves entertaining customers. However, here are four ways around the Taxman's strict rule that you can use for different occasions.

1. Give and take

Entertaining is essentially a one-sided bargain. The customer passively enjoys the hospitality, while you as the host pick up the bill. If the customer is obliged to give something in return for the hospitality, the event becomes a two-way business transaction and is not entertaining.

> *Example*
>
> *You ask customers to attend a seminar about your new product and to come armed with questions, during which you provide some glasses of wine. The customers accept the drinks as consideration for the time taken to attend and think up questions. You can deduct the cost of the wine and glass hire from your profits.*

This works with gifts too.

Example

If you give a customer a retail voucher in exchange for his used printer cartridges, which can be recycled, the customer is providing consideration in the form of the value of the empty cartridges. The voucher is not a gift as the value given by the customer is equal to the cost of the voucher.

2. Part of the trade

Where it is customary to provide complimentary refreshments as part of your normal business and the customers realise they are paying for this as part of the service, the cost of the free drinks is an allowable tax deduction.

Example

Hair salons and car dealers frequently provide complimentary tea and coffee for customers and this cost is tax deductible.

3. Incidental cost

When the hospitality is minimal to the occasion no part of the total event expenses have to be disallowed. The Taxman doesn't define what he means by minimal. In his manual he gives examples of what can't be allowed so you can argue the point if challenged.

Example

At a book launch there will normally be drinks and a cheese nibble or two provided for journalists but the main aim of the event is to promote the book. If the cost of the cheese and wine is small compared to the total event the cost of the sustenance is allowed.

4. Staff (within reason)

Entertaining your employees is tax deductible as long as it's not excessive. The Taxman also agrees that feeding non-employees who are directly involved in your business is allowable, so agency staff and self-employed contractors count towards the numbers involved in a staff meeting "over lunch".

However, the Taxman's generosity does not extend to the summer staff outing or Christmas dinner. On these occasions only current or retired staff of the company and their partners qualify, not future employees or self-employed contractors.

28.1.2. Entertaining yourself

During an enquiry the Taxman always expects to find some entertaining expenditure and looks closely at the nature of the expense incurred by the directors/employees. If, in reality, the money is being spent on entertaining personal friends, or otherwise social rather than business reasons, then the entertainment is fully taxable on the employee.

The same principles apply where a director/employee receives an allowance which is specifically intended to be spent on business entertaining. The company needs to disallow the expenditure in its computation and record the allowance on the P11D. However, the director/employee can only avoid tax to the extent that the money was spent on genuine business entertaining.

In many instances, you will incur a particular expense which the business reimburses. In this case the payment the company makes will be specifically in respect of business entertaining costs and should be disallowed in the tax computations for the business.

You can then claim a tax deduction for his expenditure on business entertainment following the general principles for making such claims, meaning you don't pay any tax on what you have reimbursed them.

28.2. WHAT ARE THE POTENTIAL TAX SAVINGS?

If you pay for entertainment out of your own pocket then it's likely that this comes out of income that has already suffered tax. If it's income from your company this money has probably been extracted as either salary or dividends. If you can reduce your tax bill by getting the company to pay direct then you are in a winning situation.

Example

In a company the entertaining add-back for Corporation Tax (CT) is at, say, a CT rate of 19%. This produces additional tax of only £190 per £1,000 of entertaining spend. As a higher rate taxpayer paying for entertainment out of dividends gives a tax cost of £250 per £1,000 and out of salary £694 per £1,000. The greater the difference between your effective rate of tax and the CT rate of your company then the more tax you'll save by the company incurring the disallowable expenditure instead of you.

28.3. THE PAPERWORK

28.3.1. Contract with/invoice from the supplier

Where possible get the invoices concerning entertainment costs to be contracted for and paid direct by your company. This avoids the reimbursed expenses hassle with P11Ds, etc.

28.3.2. On the VAT return

Your company can't claim VAT back on the purely entertaining element of any invoice. But it can apportion an invoice between, say, entertaining and subsistence and claim back the VAT on the latter.

Remember, gifts are not business entertainment, which means you can claim the input VAT back on them; provided they are less than £50 each (excluding VAT).

Tɪᴘ. Don't forget, as a VAT registered trader your company can go back three years to claim VAT you incur on its gifts if it hasn't done so already.

> *Example*
>
> *Catherine ran a successful marketing business and each year sent her valued customers a nice bottle of wine or port valued at between £20 and £30. A few years ago she wanted to know if she could claim the VAT back on their purchase so she entered "wine" into the search engine on the VATman's website and it came back with the answer "business entertainment", on which the recovery of input VAT is blocked.*
>
> *However, other rules allow the recovery of VAT on the purchase of business gifts. The even better news is that no output VAT is due when you give them away provided the total value of business gifts to each recipient does not exceed £50 (excluding VAT) in any twelve-month period. Obviously the VATman expects you to choose the perfect "phrase" when using his search engine - in this case "business gifts" not "wine".*
>
> *So Catherine could claim all the VAT back on her business gifts over the past three years and there was no output tax to pay. Her reclaim through her VAT return ended up at nearly £2,000.*

28.3.3. On your P11D

On your P11D your company has to indicate whether or not the cost of any reimbursed entertaining will be disallowed in its tax computations. So in the *Expense Payments* section of the P11D (section O) sub heading *Entertainment* don't just record the reimbursed expenses amount, tick the box too (just in front of it). Otherwise the Taxman will assume the amount is taxable on you.

These special rules relating to entertaining expenses apply to all employees, not just those with P11Ds. Where appropriate record these reimbursed expenses on P9Ds (at heading A1 Expenses Payments).

28.3.4. In the company's accounts

It may seem obvious but book entertainment costs to "entertaining".

The total "entertaining" figure per your company's accounts (from the detailed profit and loss account) needs to be added back to your company's profits in its Corporation Tax computation.

28.3.5. Your tax return

You simply take the figure given to you by the company on your P11D for "entertainment payments" and put this on your tax return. Then record a counter claim (within the same employment pages) that these were incurred by reason of your employment.

28.4. LOW, MEDIUM AND HIGH-RISK STRATEGIES

28.4.1. Low-risk

By being imaginative you can use the Taxman's own Business Income Manual against him. As a rule of thumb entertainment costs which are customary to your trade or incidental to an event should be allowable.

Remember to tick the box on the P11D to confirm that entertaining expenses will be disallowed in the business's tax computation. Otherwise the Taxman can assume these are fully taxable on you.

If you get the paperwork right the low-risk strategy is the one outlined above.

28.4.2. Medium-risk

You get assessed personally for entertainment payments as if they were income, because the Taxman doesn't accept that the expense is "wholly and exclusively" for the purpose of the company's trade. This would be the case if facts showed that the rationale behind incurring the expense is found to be personal not business, during an enquiry.

28.4.3. High-risk

If, in reality, company money is being spent on entertaining personal friends, or otherwise for social rather than business reasons, then the entertainment is fully taxable on you. The Taxman can go back up to six years to work out how much NI and tax is owed if he discovers you have been doing this. With interest on top, this could mean the company ends up facing quite a bill.

29. Computer equipment

29.1. THE EXPENSE

Computer equipment plays such an important part of modern life that it's not just confined to the workplace. Whether it's for gaming, the children's schoolwork or communicating with friends or family on the other side of the world, the majority of households now possess at least one computer. But with technological change becoming increasingly rapid, maintaining up-to-date systems can be difficult and expensive. It would be nice to let your company foot the bill.

Things were fine until April 5, 2006 because an employer was able to lend a computer to an employee for entirely private use at home and there was no taxable benefit - provided the computer cost no more than £2,500 or, if it was leased, the rental was no more than £500 a year. In fact if you're still using this equipment the exemption still applies. However, any computer equipment provided to you by your company from April 6, 2006 for private use is now chargeable to tax as a benefit-in-kind each year.

Memory sticks

Computer users have long complained that for backing up files, 3-inch floppy disks are too unstable, the ZIP drive not practical and CDs not portable enough. One of the answers to these complaints is the memory stick, which is small, portable and a very stable data storage device. Ideal for quickly backing up and restoring company computer files in the office or at home.

In future get the company to buy the memory sticks and then hand them out. If your company has a policy of writing off all fixed assets under, say £100, then there's no need to add this hardware to the fixed asset record in your accounts. They can be written off straight to computer expenses in your profit and loss account to get an immediate tax deduction for the company.

29.2. WHAT IT MIGHT COST

The benefit-in-kind for the company lending you a computer for private use is measured as 20% of its market value when first provided or the lease rental charge if higher. Remember, companies pay 12.8% Class 1A NI on benefits-in-kind.

> *Example*
>
> *The computer you've got at home is fast becoming obsolete and you decide to upgrade it with some new equipment. The system you really want, with all the peripherals, comes to £1,500. Tax on benefit of £300 (£1,500 x 20%) at 40% income tax £120. Employers' NI on benefits £300 x 12.8% = £38.*
>
> *However, the company is able to claim back the VAT whereas you aren't. VAT reclaim £1,500 x 17.5/117.5 = £223.40.*
>
> *Example*
>
> *Spending £39.99 on a 512MB memory stick and claiming it through your tax return as an expense of employment would save you income tax of £8.79 (at 22%) or £15.99 (at 40%). However, you are still out of pocket by some £31.20 or £24.00 respectively. If you've already personally bought a memory stick (and still have the receipt) then charge this to your company to get your full cost back. This is more tax efficient than trying to claim it back through your own tax return.*

29.3. WHAT ARE THE POTENTIAL TAX SAVINGS?

If you pay for the IT equipment yourself it will come from income that's already had tax deducted from it. However, if the company pays then you save some of the tax that you would have paid on that income withdrawal. The potential savings are examined below.

29.3.1. Savings on your salary

If the company pays for your IT equipment, the payments will be taxed under the benefit-in-kind rules on you as the director/employee of the company. Computer equipment is chargeable to tax as a benefit-in-kind each year, measured as 20% of the market value of the computer when first provided or the lease rental charge if higher. Employers pay 12.8% Class 1A NI on benefits-in-kind.

The tax on this benefit will be less than the tax you would have normally paid under PAYE to get the same net amount of income to make the purchase yourself. In addition there won't be any employees' NI to pay.

The company will have an NI bill to pay, but once again it will be on a lesser amount than the salary equivalent.

Example

Your company buys a computer package costing £1,500 (including VAT). It lends it to you to use at home for personal computing. How is this cheaper tax wise than buying it yourself?

29.3.2. You

	22% TAXPAYER	40% TAXPAYER
Tax on salary £1,500 (x 33 / 67) or (x 41 / 59)	739	1,042
Tax on £1,500 dividend	-	375
Tax on benefit of £300 (£1,500 x 20%)	66	120

For a 40% taxpayer the highest tax saving comes from taking a benefit-in-kind.

29.3.3. Your company and NI

	22% TAXPAYER	40% TAXPAYER
NI on salary @12.8%	287	325
NI on dividend	-	-
NI on benefits £300 @ 12.8%	38	38

29.3.4. VAT

The company is able to claim back the VAT whereas you aren't. The VAT reclaim in this example is worth £1,500 x 17.5/117.5 = £223.40.

29.4. THE PAPERWORK

By taking the following steps you will be making sure that there is no room for a challenge by the Taxman. And with all the paperwork done correctly there should be no risk of penalties arising at a later date either.

29.4.1. The board minute

Remember any expense charged in the company's accounts has to meet the "wholly and exclusively" test that we talked about earlier. Getting a formal board minute drawn up demonstrates to the Taxman that the benefit was agreed on by the company as a way of rewarding you for your services to the company. There is no need for any special wording, just a statement of the facts as a record for future reference.

Example

"Meeting of the Board of Directors of XYZ Limited on.... at...

It was resolved that the company approve the purchase of IT equipment for .... to the value of .... [amount] as part of their remuneration package.

This award has been made in recognition of their continuing contribution to the success of the company.

Signed .... company secretary."

29.4.2. Contract of employment

Because this is a variation of your remuneration package you will need to incorporate it into your contract of employment by way of an addendum.

Example

"As of .... the company will pay for new IT equipment to the value of .... [amount] for your own personal use. This benefit-in-kind is to be treated as part of your remuneration package with the company."

29.4.3. Contract with/invoice from the supplier

Getting the supplier to invoice the company will make it absolutely clear that the liability for payment belongs with the company and not you.

29.4.4. On the VAT return

As the contract is with the company, any VAT charged on the purchase of the computer equipment can be reclaimed on your company's VAT return.

29.4.5. On your P11D

The value of the benefit-in-kind to be included is 20% of the total cost of the equipment before the deduction of VAT.

29.4.6. In the company's accounts

There are no special disclosure requirements, the IT equipment gets lost in the fixed asset additions total shown in the accounts.

29.4.7. On your tax return

Simply transfer the values from your P11D to the relevant boxes on your tax return's employment pages. Any tax due will then be collected in the normal way.

29.5. LOW, MEDIUM AND HIGH-RISK STRATEGIES

29.5.1. Low-risk

Getting the paperwork right as described above cuts all risk down to an absolute minimum.

Buy memory sticks for your employees (including yourself) for back up purposes. This is more tax efficient than an employee buying the storage and then trying to claim it back for tax.

29.5.2. Medium-risk

If it's unclear that the payment is part of your remuneration package there's a risk that the company won't be allowed a deduction in the accounts under the "true and fair" rules. This means a loss of Corporation Tax relief.

29.5.3. High-risk

A high-risk strategy here would be for the company to pay for the equipment without declaring anything to the Taxman about its private use. You will get away with paying no tax on the benefits and having the tax relief on the purchase. However, if discovered, the Taxman will hit the company with a bill for the tax and NI unpaid. In addition, there will be the fines for incorrect P11Ds and interest for late payment of tax due.

30. Technical notes

These notes supplement the other chapters in this book. They incorporate references to statutory and other authorities, and the abbreviations used are those conventionally adopted by taxation advisors.

For example, the **Income Tax (Employment and Pensions) Act** is abbreviated to "**ITEPA**" and the **Taxman's Employment Income Manual** to "**EIM**".

References to "the Taxman" is our shorthand for HM Revenue & Customs (HMRC). And a reference to married couples includes same-sex couples who have registered under the **Civil Partnership Act 2004**.

Our references to paragraphs in the Taxman's own manuals can be followed up by visiting http://www.hmrc.gov.uk/manuals/.

1. INTRODUCTION

<u>Wholly and exclusively</u>

BIM37035 - for the statutory prohibition, which is "expenditure must be incurred wholly and exclusively for purposes of the trade".

But what does "the purposes of the trade" mean?

For a company. The purpose for which a company spends money can only be the purpose of the directors or the shareholders (in the latter instance, if such purpose is expressed at a general meeting). **Morgan v Tate and Lyle Ltd (1954).**

Company law. Directors' remuneration is determined by the shareholders at their Annual General Meeting, not the Taxman. The shareholders decide what is necessary for the company's trade.

2. CLAIMING THROUGH YOUR COMPANY

The Taxman publishes a whole series of guides that relate to the rules for claiming expenses. **480 - Expenses and Benefits - A tax guide; 490 - Employee Travel - A tax and NICs guide for employers.** So, genuine business expense claims are tax deductible but also strictly monitored by the Taxman.

Dispensations

http://www.hmrc.gov.uk/employers/moretma-ebik.shtml.

Authorising your own expense claims

In the Taxman's own words **(EIM30053)** *"Employers should be encouraged to apply for dispensations where appropriate"*. Furthermore, the guidance tells the Taxman to *"Give dispensations that are applied for whenever the criteria for giving them are met"* and confirms that *"Dispensations should not be limited to large firms. Give them regardless of the number of employees to be covered."* Therefore all is not lost. If the Taxman seems reluctant to grant a dispensation remind him of the words in **EIM30053**.

Employer paying employee's debt: the pecuniary liability principle

A benefit counts as earnings under **s.62 ITEPA 2003** if it is money's worth. Money's worth includes things that are of direct monetary value to the employee.

An example of this is where the employer pays a debt that the employee owes to a third party. This is often called the pecuniary liability principle. The employer's payment is of direct monetary value to the employee because he or she no longer has to pay that amount of money to the third party. It therefore counts as money's worth under **s.62 (3)(a) ITEPA 2003**. It will be taxable as earnings if it comes from the employment **(EIM00580)**.

Liability will depend upon who enters into the contract with the party supplying the goods or services. You therefore need to establish exactly what the particular contractual arrangements are in order to determine who has entered into the contract. It is not enough to rely upon identifying who the bill is addressed to since this only concerns who is to pay the bill. The address on the bill does not have any bearing on who contracted for the supply/provision of the goods or services. **(NIM02270.)**

By reason of employment

EIM21600 - the benefits code.

3. UNINCORPORATED BUSINESSES

BIM37007 - wholly and exclusively overview.

Private use adjustments

As we mentioned earlier, the Taxman's rulebook is deafeningly silent on the subject of apportionment. What it does say, however, is that he will try to penalise anyone who is obviously trying it on.

EIM31662 - decided cases in which apportionment was permitted.

The practice of apportioning expenditure where a definite part can be identified as incurred wholly and exclusively for a particular purpose has been approved by the courts e.g. **Caillebotte v Quinn**.

4. DEALING WITH THE TAXMAN

Taxman: Expenses and benefits-in-kind: quick guide to whether tax and NICs are due http://www.hmrc.gov.uk/employers/ebik/ebik2/table-of-contents.htm.

The list is intended to cover the expenses and benefits commonly provided and describes the right way to deal with expenses and benefits where you do not have a dispensation.

Booklet 480 - Expenses & Benefits - A tax guide
http://www.hmrc.gov.uk/guidance/480.htm.

Marginal cost

Pepper v Hart (HL 1992). Applying the Pepper v Hart principle, the value of the benefit is the marginal cost to you of providing the goods/services. For example, this would be the cost of purchasing the goods, plus any costs that vary in accordance with the quantity of goods purchased, for example, delivery charges, etc. However, you don't need to take account of fixed costs, such as rent etc.

5. USE OF HOME BY A COMPANY

The £2 a week

When an employee works at home for some or all of the time, he or she may incur additional household costs, for example in heating and lighting. The employer may make payments to the employee tax-free and without any liability for NICs to help to meet those additional costs.

The employer can pay up to £2 per week (£104 per year) without obtaining any supporting evidence of the additional costs **(s.316A ITEPA 2003)**. The employer can pay more than that where evidence is retained to show that the amount paid is no greater than the additional costs incurred by the employee.

Scale rate payments that reimburse the average expenses met by employees working at home can be paid tax-free and without any liability for NICs if the amount has been agreed by a Tax Inspector.

Tax Bulletin 79 http://www.hmrc.gov.uk/bulletins/tb79.htm#a "Employees Who Work At Home - Tax Relief For Unreimbursed Homeworking Expenses - **s.336 ITEPA 2003**".

This superseded the guidance on working from home and household expenses which appeared at **EIM32760** onwards.

Rent

Where an employer claims that the payment to an employee is rent chargeable on the employee as property income then this is tax deductible for the company and not earnings of the employee. **(EIM01400.)**

6. GARDEN MAINTENANCE

In order to manage the business a company has to attract and retain key employees. The cost of this usually meets the "wholly and exclusively" test, provided it's not excessive for the duties performed. Therefore, if you reassess your remuneration package (as an employee) to include in it say garden maintenance that you want your company to incur (as a benefit-in kind for yourself) this is, in our opinion, "wholly and exclusively for the purposes of the trade" too. However, if challenged on this "part of your remuneration" argument by the Taxman you'll need to be able to provide him with a copy of what was agreed in writing.

National minimum wage (NMW)

The remuneration defence against a "wholly and exclusively" attack relies on you actually having a contract of employment with your company. According to DTI guidance the NMW will apply to directors if they have a contract of employment, as this makes them workers.

7. GIFTS

Gifts not taxable as earnings

A gift does not count as earnings within **s.62 ITEPA 2003** if it is made:

- on personal grounds (for example, a wedding present) or
- as a mark of personal esteem or appreciation.

(EIM01460)

If the gift is a genuine one - that is, a personal and unexpected gift made from an employer to an employee, given as a gesture of goodwill or as a token of gratitude - the payment is not earnings and, therefore, no NI is due. **(NIM02165.)**

Trivial benefits

You can ask for a benefit to be exempt from tax on the grounds that the cash equivalent of the benefit taxable on the employee is so trivial as to be not worth pursuing. **(EIM21860.)** Examples of trivial benefits can be found at **EIM21863**.

Annual parties and other social functions

Directors and employees are chargeable on their share of the expense incurred by an employer in providing a social function for employees, except where **s.264 ITEPA 2003** exempts the charge to tax **(EIM21690)**. The exemption applies to an annual party (for example, a Christmas party), or similar annual function (for example, a summer barbecue), provided for employees and is:

- available to employees generally or
- available to employees generally at one location, where the employer has more than one location.

NOTE. In practice (if they spot it) local inspectors have been known to argue that this expense is not for the purpose of the business in husband and wife companies and thus not give a Corporation Tax deduction or try to assess the amounts as taxable. This is on the basis that you will think it costs too much to challenge him and so will back down. If he would allow it for larger companies ask him why he is discriminating against your company.

8. LANGUAGE LESSONS

Your company can get a full tax deduction for any work-related training it provides to its employees, which includes you as a director **(s.250 ITEPA 2003)**. "Work-related" means any skill the employee may have need of at work either now or in the future, or even when the employee works in a voluntary capacity on behalf of the firm, such as helping a local charity.

See also **EIM01210**.

9. MAGAZINE SUBSCRIPTIONS

EIM32880 - professional fees and subscriptions.

s.343 and **s.344 ITEPA 2003.**

10. PAYING FOR A HOLIDAY

A benefit provided for a member of an employee's family or household, whether by his employer or someone else, is chargeable on him under the benefits code if it is provided by reason of his employment. If the benefit is provided by the employee's employer it is deemed to be provided by reason of the employment **(s.201(3) ITEPA 2003** and **EIM20502)**.

"Family or household" **(s.721(5) ITEPA 2003)** means:

- the employee's spouse or (from December 5, 2005) civil partner
- the employee's children and their spouses or (from December 5, 2005) civil partners
- the employee's parents
- the employee's dependants
- the employee's domestic staff
- the employee's guests (that is people staying at his invitation in his home or in accommodation provided by him).

Thus an employee who takes his family away on holiday at his employer's expense is chargeable not only on the cost of his own holiday fares and accommodation but also on the cost of those relating to his wife and family.

11. PRIVATE TUTORS

Before April 6, 2005 childcare vouchers couldn't be used to pay for any form of education, but the law now says that the qualifying care can be any form of care or supervised activity that is not part of the child's compulsory education **(s.318B(1) ITEPA 2003)**. So as long as the subject of your child's extra lessons is not covered in compulsory school hours, in his or her particular school, it can be paid for directly by your company or with childcare vouchers up to the tax-free limit.

The second condition for the childcare to be tax and NI-free, is that it must be provided by a registered or approved childcarer.

12. SCHOOL FEES

The trick is to get the educational establishment to agree to contract directly with your company so that the company is liable to pay the fees in all circumstances. In this case, you can avoid paying employees' NI - a saving of up to 11% of the cost of the fees.

In the case of **Frost Skip Hire (Newcastle) Ltd v IRC SpC (2004)**, the company had agreed with the school to pay the fees of the director's son. Invoices for fees due were rendered to the company, which paid them. However, it was the parents, not the company, who signed the original school entry forms that contained terms and conditions making them personally liable for the fees. There was no evidence of any renegotiation of contracts between the company and the school. So it was deemed that the company was meeting a liability of the parents and both employers' and employees' NI was due on the total fees paid.

Even if you get all the paperwork right so the contract is genuinely between the school/university and the company, you will still be taxed on the fees paid as a benefit-in-kind. The company is paying the school fees because you are its employee. This was shown in the case **Glyn v CIR (Hong Kong) 1990**. The company had agreed in the taxpayer's contract of employment to pay his child's boarding school fees while he worked in Hong Kong. The school fees were held to be part of the taxpayer's total remuneration package and were taxable as a benefit-in-kind. As long as you can justify the level of remuneration for work done.

See **Expenses and benefits-in-kind: quick guide to whether tax and NICs are due: school fees** for the Taxman's summary for this expense http://www.hmrc.gov.uk/employers/ebik/ebik2/school-fees.htm.

13. PERSONAL TRAINER

To obtain a tax deduction in the company your argument is that the contract with the personal trainer is within "the benefits code" and hence is part of your employment income. This is best taken care of by adding the provision by the company of a personal trainer to your contract of employment.

Liability will depend upon who enters into the contract with the party supplying the goods or services. The address on the bill does not have any bearing on who contracted for the supply/provision of the goods or services. **(NIM02270.)**

14. CARS FOR THE FAMILY

Members of your family or household are defined at **EIM20504**.

15. WINE

Again the tax bill will depend upon who enters into the contract with the party supplying the goods or services. The address on the bill does not have any bearing on who contracted for the supply/provision of the goods or services. **(NIM02270.)**

Not for bonuses

A series of high profile schemes for paying bonuses in assets that would sizeably appreciate in value (such as gold coins, gold jewellery, gold bars, platinum sponge, trade debts, coffees beans, fine wine and oriental carpets) has resulted in anti-avoidance legislation in this area. However, such provisions should not catch fine wines for your own consumption, acquired through a wine club.

16. COMPANY PLANE (OR YACHT)

Aeroplane

For the Taxman's valuation of the benefit-in-kind for private use of a company aeroplane see the example at **EIM21638**.

EIM21637 - mixed (private v business) use assets placed at the disposal of a director or employee.

CA27300 - assets used partly for a qualifying activity.

Yacht

For the Taxman's valuation of the benefit-in-kind for private use of a company yacht see the example at **EIM21633**.

s.205 ITEPA 2003.

17. GYM MEMBERSHIP

An employer can pay a club membership fee for directors or employees. The expense incurred will be a benefit chargeable on directors and employees **(EIM21696)**. If you pay a composite subscription entitling all employees to membership, liability arises on directors and employees who are not lower paid (more than £8,500 p.a. including the value of any benefits). Any reasonable apportionment of the total subscription cost amongst employees should be accepted. **(EIM01060.)**

Club membership is mainly a personal and social matter, giving rise to amenities and privileges limited to members. Any suggestion that the cost of membership of a club is deductible as a necessary expense incurred in the performance of the duties of the employment would normally be rejected by the Taxman **(EIM32500)**. Therefore, to obtain a tax deduction in the company your argument is that the membership fee is paid by an employer for a director or employee within "the benefits code" as part of your contract of employment.

<u>The exemption route</u>

No charge on earnings as employment income arises from the provision by employers for employees, former employees or members of their families or households of:

- qualifying sports or recreational facilities **(s.261(2) ITEPA 2003)**, or

- non-cash vouchers exchangeable only for the use of such facilities.

A qualifying sports or recreational benefit or facility is one that:

- is available generally to all the employees of the employer concerned **(s.261(3)** - facilities provided for a few, selected employees only do not qualify) and

- is not available to members of the public generally **(s.261(4))**

- is used wholly or mainly by employees or former employees and members of their families or household **(s.261(5))**.

(EIM21825.)

18. GARAGE STORAGE

Any allowance paid to you for use of your garage by your company counts as earnings. Therefore PAYE should be applied to the payment. This will be the case whether or not the garage is attached to your home **(s.62 ITEPA 2003 and EIM01400)**.

Where an employer claims that the payment to an employee is rent chargeable on the employee as property income then this is tax deductible for the company and not earnings of the employee. **(EIM01400.)**

Case law: **Beecham Group v Fair (1983)** - where PAYE needs to be applied.

19. NANNIES

Liability will depend upon who enters into the contract with the party supplying the goods or services. The address on the bill does not have any bearing on who contracted for the supply/provision of the goods or services. **(NIM02270.)**

20. PETTY CASH DIFFERENCES

Round sum allowances

EIM05100 - Employment income: round sum expense allowances.

s.62 ITEPA 2003.

NIM06160.

21. THE WEEKEND AWAY

s.337 to s.339 ITEPA 2003.

EIM31811 - expenses do not have to be "wholly and exclusively" incurred: example.

EIM31815 - associated subsistence.

EIM31820 and **EIM02710** other incidental costs/expenses.

EIM31950 - overseas conferences, seminars and study tours.

22. DOMESTIC HELP

An employer may provide domestic help, in the form of paying for chefs, cleaners etc.

s.62 ITEPA 2003.

Booklet 480 paras. 4.3 and 21.7.

The domestic help needs to be genuinely self-employed to avoid the risk of these payments later being classed made to "employees" of the company, with additional tax and NI bills.

Liability will depend upon who enters into the contract with the party supplying the goods or services. The address on the bill does not have any bearing on who contracted for the supply/provision of the goods or services. **(NIM02270.)**

23. TAXI FARES

Where transport home from a permanent workplace is provided by an employer on no more than 60 days in any one year because of exceptional late night working or the failure of car sharing arrangements, this is exempt from tax under **s.248 ITEPA 2003**. (See also **EIM21731**.)

24. OVERNIGHT ALLOWANCE

Scale rate payments

EIM05200 - scale rate expenses payments.

NIM05680 - scale rates based on an estimate of costs.

NIM06170 - NI and scale rate payments.

To download a PDF copy of the Taxman's **Film Industry Guidance Notes** visit http://www.hmrc.gov.uk/specialist/film_industry.htm. Within the PDF section 10 "Tax treatment of expenses" contains the generous figures for accommodation allowances etc.

Personal incidental expenses

EIM02710 and **EIM02730** - incidental overnight expenses.

s.240 and s.241 ITEPA 2003.

NIM06010.

25. USE OF THE COMPANY VILLA

Living accommodation: meaning of provided

The cash equivalent value of the benefit from living accommodation that is "provided" for an employee is taxable. The meaning of provided is often an issue in the case of holiday accommodation. It is not defined in the legislation and its meaning has not been considered by the courts in this context. So the word is given its ordinary dictionary meaning by the Taxman: supplied or furnished with a thing. In some cases provided will mean available for use whereas in others it will mean actually used.

In deciding whether "provided" means available for use, or means actually used, the following questions will be asked by the Taxman **(EIM11406)**.

- Who can use the living accommodation? The Taxman accepts that if living accommodation is genuinely available for use by more people than could actually use it at any one time then provided only means the periods actually used. For example if five unrelated employees were allowed to use an employer owned two bedroom holiday villa we would only seek a provided living accommodation charge on each employee for the period in which that employee actually used the villa.

- Why was the living accommodation bought or rented and how has it been used since acquisition? If the living accommodation was bought as holiday accommodation for a director and family, provided is likely to mean available for use. By contrast if it was bought as a genuine letting business by the employer and has been let out commercially then provided will only mean the periods of actual use by the employee.

For examples illustrating these points see **EIM11421**.

26. ADVISORS' FEES

No special legislation relating to these fees. The charge to tax is therefore under either **s.62 ITEPA 2003** or under the benefits code.

Case law: **Pepper v hart (1992)**.

EIM13740 and **Esc A81** - legal fees regarding termination of employment.

27. PARKING NEAR WORK

There is no tax charge **(s.237 ITEPA 2003)** on a director or employee within the benefits code on the provision of a car or motorcycle parking space at or near his place of work. Facilities for parking bicycles are also exempt. **(EIM21685.)**

28. ENTERTAINING

Where you contract with the provider of the entertainment and your company pays or reimburses you, you need to be able to support that request with reasonable records of the amounts spent on particular occasions, the nature of the entertainment, the persons entertained and the reasons for the entertainment **(see EIM32615 and NIM05670)**.

29. COMPUTER EQUIPMENT

Annual value

EIM21632 - 20% of annual value.

When an employee is provided with a benefit by the transfer of the ownership of an asset, the cost of the benefit (this is called the "cash equivalent") is normally the expense incurred by the person providing the benefit, less any amount made good by the employee. If an employee earning at a rate of £8,500 a year or more has an asset placed at their disposal, without any transfer of ownership, there are special rules for the amount of the benefit charge. The cash equivalent is equal to 20% of the market value of the computer when it was first supplied to the employee plus any running costs met by the employer in the year.

The market value of an asset at a particular time is defined **(s.208 ITEPA 2003)** as the price that it might reasonably have been expected to fetch on a sale in the open market at that time.